A MIND AT EASE

ROBERT LIDDELL

A Mind at Ease

Barbara Pym and Her Novels

PETER OWEN · LONDON

ISBN 0 7206 0731 0

PETER OWEN PUBLISHERS
73 Kenway Road London SW5 0RE

First published in Great Britain 1989
© Robert Liddell 1989
Typeset by Photosetting & Secretarial Services Yeovil
Printed in Great Britain by Billings of Worcester

Contents

A mind lively and at ease, can do with seeing nothing, and can see nothing that does not answer.

Jane Austen

An Apology

These pages are intended as a critical survey of those works of Barbara Pym which were prepared by herself for publication. Three were indeed published after her death, but *A Few Green Leaves* had been revised by her. *Crampton Hodnet* and *An Unsuitable Attachment* are included because the author had in fact offered them for publication, though I believe that she would finally have rejected them, and that she would have done well to do so.

My purpose to present her as a worthwhile author is essentially critical rather than scholarly, and I therefore confine myself to the work on which I feel sure her reputation must rest. Those who wish to know more (and there can hardly be a more fully documented author) will find all that can be known admirably presented by her devoted and tireless executor Hazel Holt.

A question that I have been asked, and can only attempt to answer is: 'What has caused her immense popularity since she has been rediscovered?' First, I believe that her rediscovery could have happened much sooner (if less sensationally) had publishers been more enterprising. Some of their readers had appreciated her work, and she was never without a faithful public.

Next, I think that the inspiration that went into her first books ('the canon') was in decline, and that *An Unsuitable Attachment* merited its rejection. Barbara needed two or three years' pause between 1960 and 1963; she had temporarily written herself out.

Third, I think the disappointing 1970s prepared a reading public for domestic and slightly old-fashioned work – just as the Second

World War made Anthony Trollope an immensely popular author again.

Lastly, I believe that a change was needed from novels too full of sociology or sex. The 'acquittal' of Lady Chatterley encouraged some writers to make excessive use of the liberty they had gained, and very tedious many of them were in consequence – while the absorption of so much of the reading public into the middle class made the 'socially conscious' novel almost anachronistic.

Another question, but perhaps unanswerable, is: 'What is the secret of her spell?' Her books often seem to come to us like gifts of nature, like the air we breathe or the water we drink (but purer and more wholesome). I do not know what a critic would find to say about them if others had not been in the field before him, and had made errors that needed correction – there would be little to do except to tell the stories of the novels (though even that task demands judgement and accuracy).

ABBREVIATIONS

EW	*Excellent Women*
FGL	*A Few Green Leaves*
GB	*A Glass of Blessings*
JP	*Jane and Prudence*
LA	*Less than Angels*
NFR	*No Fond Return of Love*
QA	*Quartet in Autumn*
STG	*Some Tame Gazelle*
SDD	*The Sweet Dove Died*
UA	*An Unsuitable Attachment*

ONE

The Early Years

[1]

Some Tame Gazelle

The Bodleian Library in Oxford is too well known to need description, but even in that august building there have been temporary changes and arrangements from time to time. During the 1930s an open access reading-room was provided on the east side of the Old Schools quadrangle, where those reading for the School of English Language and Literature had ready to hand most of the books they were likely to require. The English Reading Room could be entered from the south through the picture gallery, or from the north through the Upper Reading Room (largely devoted to catalogues and learned periodicals) and the Tower Room, where publications deemed obscene were kept under lock and key – a previous librarian had humorously bestowed on them the Greek letter phi (Φ) as a press-mark.

Barbara Pym, a first-year undergraduate of St Hilda's College, came here often in the summer term of 1932 to prepare her essays. She was a cheerful, romantic, outgoing girl of just nineteen, playfully flirtatious, whose interest in men was keen but not obsessive. It was perhaps unfortunate for her that at another desk sat Henry Harvey, a second-year man from Christ Church, with whom she became rather more deeply involved than usual. If unfortunate for her, it was fortunate for me – he was a great friend of mine, otherwise it was unlikely that I should have met her. She called him 'Lorenzo', perhaps from 'The Pot of Basil', perhaps from the character in Young's 'Night Thoughts', or perhaps just because she liked the name; she adopted 'Cassandra' for her own.

She felt emboldened to drop a note on his desk at the end of the term, but it was not until the next academic year that their friendship at all ripened, and I hardly met Barbara till I was sharing a flat with Henry in the Banbury Road from September 1933. By then I was on the staff of the Bodleian, in the Department of Western Manuscripts; Henry had taken his degree, and was preparing a thesis for BLitt.; and Barbara was in her last year.

She sometimes visited us, unchaperoned, during the following summer, and Henry read poetry aloud to her, which he was very fond of doing. She was a patient and devoted listener. She and I had two inexhaustible subjects of conversation: 'Eng. Lit.', in which her reading was wide and sometimes eccentric, covering a number of minor poets from the seventeenth century onwards, and 'C of E'. Though I was already a Catholic, I retained a great affection for the Church of my baptism, my kindly nurse – and even had some nostalgia for its beauty and cosiness. Barbara and I delighted in the vagaries of clergy of all denominations in a way that, I am sure, was disrespectful, though I hope it was not irreverent. The Bodleian itself also provided plenty to talk about, and Barbara with her detective instinct liked knowing about all our friends and acquaintances.

In September 1934 Henry went to Finland, as lector in the University of Helsingfors, and my brother Donald came from Cambridge to share my flat. Barbara had gone down, and often wrote to me from Oswestry. It was that Christmas that I sent her the select poems of Rochester ('the dear earl', she called him). It professed to be *a collection of such pieces only, as may be received in a vertuous court, and may not unbecome the Cabinet of the Severest Matron* – and I accompanied it with the following poem.

> Cassandra in the library by turn
> Would con her book, or for Lorenzo burn.
> Small help it was to reason with herself
> When the great poets cried from every shelf

And with one universal voice approved
Her flame. Small wonder that Cassandra loved.
The mighty schoolman in the stall of Inge
First gravely argued: 'Since the end's the thing
By which each action must be justified:
The right true end of love....' With angry pride
No sooner had the Nymph rejected clean
The wicked promptings of the gloomy Dean
Than two more learned men in haste begin
Basely to tempt her down the path of sin.
By Master Cleveland's muse instructed, she
Exclaims: 'Give me a lover bold and free.'
Then, blushing and repentant, in a trice
She hies for absolution and advice
To Master Herrick, who can only say:
'Gather ye rosebuds, virgins, while ye may.'
She left these gentle turtles to their cooing,
Only to meet a more tremendous wooing.
Beholding her, the godlike Puritan
Forgot his godhead, and became a man,
And prayed her as a second Eve to come
And share his Eden in Elysium.
Where he, John Milton, she, Cassandra Pym,
(He for God only, she for God in him),
Might live again the early days of Earth –
Unwieldy elephants should give them Mirth,
Only no serpent should be lurking there.
Cassandra, having no desire to share
The simple pleasures of that garden state,
Flung down her book, and rushed precipitate
To find a shelter in the Tower's cell –
Praying St Barbara to shield her well.
But all the raucous myrmidons of Phi
At her arrival lifted up their cry.
My good Lord Rochester was at her feet,

With propositions that I daren't repeat.
Havelock Ellis put her on her guard
Against th'intentions of the Comte de Sade.
Sure of success, poor Casanova's hopes
Were dashed to pieces by a word from Stopes.
From this unholy rabble, in retreat
Cassandra hastened to her country seat.
There, calm and safe, amid domestic joys,
The household care her busy hands employs.
While in her leisure hours she reads what's writ
Only by poets of the chastest wit.
Go, little book, purged of all grosser stains,
Where only poetry and truth remains.
Attend upon her like an eunuch page
Upon a lady of declining age.
Whisper her words of peace and sweet content,
And wish her CALM OF MIND, ALL PASSION SPENT.

These lines, I think, well enough reflect the character of our friendship.

Barbara's letters to me have a further interest. In July she had begun a novel about herself and her sister Hilary as 'Belinda and Harriet Bede', spinsters of about fifty. Chapters of this novel (which ultimately became *Some Tame Gazelle*) were frequently sent to me.

This seems the best place to discuss the chronology of the book's composition and that of its story.

The manuscript went through several recensions.

First, there was the manuscript as I saw it. No doubt I made a few suggestions, but the most important was that she should delete passages about Nazis in exile in South Africa. Barbara had lately been in Germany and had a charming admirer, Friedbert, who gave her a swastika, though she had no Nazi affiliations. However, though myself also politically rather naïve and innocent, I felt that Barbara had overdone it. It seemed to me a good thing that the

Nazis should be in exile, and that they were not worthy objects of the Misses Bedes' charity – but most of all I objected to the element of an imaginary future, which would have been damaging to the structure and chronology of the main story.

Second, the manuscript, after some correction, was unsucessfully offered to several publishers. In August 1936 Jonathan Cape wrote that he might be able to publish it if a few alterations were made.

Third, Jonathan Cape, 'falser than false Cressid', rejected the revised manuscript and it remained on Barbara's hands.

Fourth, in 1945, on my return from Egypt for the summer, I called at Bedford Square. Jonathan (then my publisher) said (incorrectly, as it happened), 'You introduced two very attractive young women to me. One of them had written a novel.' He seemed to have some recollection of it.

'I am not surprised,' I said loyally. 'It is very good.'

'Tell her to revise it and send it in again,' he said.

One feature of the last revision can be identified. In 1946 Barbara began work at the International African Institute. It must be after that date that she brought in the colonial bishop with his rather philistine contempt for the technicalities of anthropology.

In 1949 the finally revised manuscript was accepted by Cape and published by him in the following year.

The book, therefore, was written or revised from 1934 till 1949. Very probably Barbara added touches now and then all through that period.

It seems that before it reached completion she had imagined the happenings as taking place about 1935. The events of the troubled years that followed have made no mark. The rather silly Nazi excursus (which she readily deleted) had been a temporary piece of self-indulgence, and is only mentioned here because it shows that at first she must have been in some doubt about chronology. Belinda and Harriet were to be 'fiftyish'. Was she to make everything happen some thirty years hence, or to antedate their birth by as many years? Wisely she took the second course. She was therefore able to write a novel about the contemporary world, simply making the characters older – for nearly all of them were in some way suggested by life. No doubt it amused her mother, then alive, to become 'our dear mother' as a hallowed memory. But one reader complained that he found the sisters rather girlish; he did not think that, in their fifties, Belinda would have watched Harriet wallowing in her bath.

The book gained by its appearance in 1950. It was about a cosier world, when people had resident servants, and there was plenty to eat – no ration cards, 'points' or queues, and cream and butter abounded. Barbara was later to write about the lean years that followed the war all the more convincingly for having known better days. Though in life there had been shadows of war, in this novel they were never present: the Archdeacon might threaten his congregation with the terrors of the Last Judgement, but these were more remote and less alarming than aerial bombardment. Any troubles of those interwar years were soothingly far away. English people always expected unpleasant conditions in 'the Balkans' – where Edith Liversidge did wonders for the sanitation; and if John Akenside were accidentally shot in Prague, was not Neville Chamberlain to speak of the Czechs as 'far away people of whom we knew nothing'?

The main interest is in Belinda's affections. By making all her characters middle-aged Barbara has found the secret of something almost unique: it is an Oxford novel (for most of the people are Oxonian) written away from Oxford, and without the banality of undergraduate loves and enthusiasms.

Belinda and Harriet Bede were snugly settled in an English village when Archdeacon Henry Hoccleve (he who had been 'Lorenzo') arrived as the new vicar. He was now married to Agatha, a sharp-featured woman based on one Alison (whom Henry had admired or had affected to admire, to tease Barbara). She was the daughter of a bishop and knowledgeable about Middle English. A very comfortable state of unrequited love now rewarded Belinda. She 'realized how well her heart, broken at twenty-five, had mended with the passing of the years'. For 'She was now a contented spinster and her love was like a warm, comfortable garment, bedsocks or even woollen combinations, certainly something without glamour or romance.'

Barbara's original 'unrequited love' for Henry had been tending this way. She had sometimes reproached me for not taking her loves seriously enough; at other times – when they had ended in tears – she found some comfort in regarding them (as I did) as a kind of game. Henry's marriage in Finland, at the end of 1937, had grieved her as putting an end to a fairy-tale; but she had no right to feel aggrieved, and was far too sensible to have done so.

By that time she had completed one recension of the novel, if not two, and knew imaginatively how passion can give way to a gentle, undemanding friendship, even if at twenty-five she had not got so far as Belinda had thirty years on. Nevertheless the example of Belinda must have helped her. It seems to be a *remedium amoris* that no one ever thought of before, probably more efficacious than the Yeastvite tablets* that Barbara took for that purpose, another original remedy.

A kind of comic underplot is provided by Harriet and her love of curates (evidently a good-natured family joke). This innocent passion is expressed in knitting them sweaters and socks (which often have to be finished by Belinda), bearing jelly or well-baked cakes to their lodgings, and entertaining them to supper frequently, and often lavishly. The book owes its title to this weakness.

> Some tame gazelle, some gentle dove:
> Something to love, oh, something to love!

So wrote Thomas Haines Bayly. And when one curate goes, sacrificed to matrimony or to the mission field, another is sure to

---

A Very Private Eye: The Diaries, Letters and Notebooks of Barbara Pym, Hazel Holt and Hilary Pym (eds), Macmillan, London, 1984.

take his place, and will do as well. The beautiful opening of the book gives the atmosphere at once:

> The new curate seemed quite a nice young man, but what a pity it was that his combinations showed, tucked carelessly into his socks, when he sat down. Belinda had noticed it when they had met him for the first time at the vicarage last week and had felt quite embarrassed. Perhaps Harriet could say something to him about it. Her blunt jolly manner could carry off these little awkwardnesses much better than Belinda's timidity. Of course he might think it was none of their business, as indeed it was not, but Belinda rather doubted whether he thought at all, if one were to judge by the quality of his first sermon.

Yet Barbara has not only contrived the solution of conceiving her love-story as thirty years on; she has gone further, turning 'Lorenzo' into a gloriously comic character – all passion is spent in laughter, or rather has 'mellowed into a comfortable feeling, more like the cosiness of a winter evening by the fire than the uncertain rapture of a spring morning'.

Every one of the 'Lorenzo's' weaknesses has been exaggerated. He is essentially a solipsist, and loves above all things the sound of his own voice (in which sometimes a faint lisp is heard), but minds very little about the patient listener, if he is reading aloud, or the congregation, if he is preaching. His famous sermon on the Judgement Day is his greatest performance. He began with quotations from seventeenth-century poetry, reading some thirty-five lines of Thomas Flatman's. The four here quoted are good.

At once we see Barbara's gift for quotation and (though this is not her purpose) we can imagine that she has enriched some readers' knowledge of English literature more subtly than much scholarship has done. Flatman was a very minor poet; once the eminent Ben Jonson scholar, Percy Simpson, met me in St Giles when he was doing some work upon that author and complained: 'I feel as if I had deserted my lawful wife for a very inferior mistress.'

[18]

But Barbara has put Flatman on the literary map.

On went the Archdeacon into the eighteenth century, when Blair promised that at the Resurrection of the body every joint should:

> possess its proper place
> With a new elegance of form unknown.

But he ended with menacing lines addressed by Edward Young to the unknown Lorenzo for whom the 'Night Thoughts' were written, evidently a far from commendable character.

He had gone on too long; many of his parishioners would return to badly over-roasted beef. Belinda believed that at the vicarage they were having duck which 'can't really be cooked too much'. The Archdeacon, however, had probably not thought of that; he expected everything to be in order in his household without any trouble on his part – though in fact Agatha was rather stingy.

In this the Archdeacon is like the typical man of Barbara's world, who depends on women to do all the disagreeable chores, and to like it: 'I thought women enjoyed missing meals and making martyrs of themselves' – and perhaps the clergy are especially likely to find women doing this for them. Agatha, however, let moths get at his best suit, and is not careful about darning his socks – not only does he let her know it, but he lets Belinda into the secret: 'I don't think *you* would have done it.' But insensitive as he is about the past, he has a nice gift for quotation, not only from the pulpit. Harriet tells him that Belinda is in bed with a chill, but has asked for the *Oxford Book of Victorian Verse*.

'She called for madder music and for stronger wine,' said the Archdeacon. He is always worth talking to.

Belinda's devotion still lived.

The fierce flame had died down, but the fire was still glowing brightly.

My very ashes in their urn
Shall like a hallowed lamp for ever burn....

How much more one appreciated our great literature if one loved, thought Belinda, especially if the love were unrequited!

On the whole the Misses Bede lived enviable lives, and could enjoy to the full the comfort of tea at home, drawn curtains, and the patter of the rain outside. It is a happy thing to remember that Barbara was later in life, though too briefly, to enjoy such cosiness with her sister in Oxfordshire.

The minor characters may be said to be suggested by life rather than drawn from it, and sometimes a very slight suggestion has been enough. Some of them may be explained by the fact that the first recension, from which they survive, was really written for Henry and me, and was hardly yet fully intended to be a novel – it was more like a serial letter and Agatha and others (some of whom we knew rather better than Barbara did) figured in it then by their own names.

John Akenside, killed accidentally while looking on at a revolution in Prague, was our friend John Barnicot, at one time in charge of the Radcliffe Camera, the chief reading-room of the Bodleian. Though prematurely dead, his memory was kept green by two people. One was his friend Count Ricardo Bianco (in life Roberto Weiss – a distinguished Renaissance scholar). In the novel he is hopelessly in love with Harriet (whose original I believe Roberto never saw) – this makes an excellent parallel with Belinda's love for the Archdeacon. Edith Liversidge, who did splendid work for sanitation in the Balkans, and is believed to have been loved by John Akenside, is based on Honor Tracy whose blunt speech and bruiser-like appearance are given to her, but not her lovely speaking voice.

Barbara elevated me, under the name of Nicholas Parnell, to the rank of Bodley's librarian and sent me there with my deputy Nathaniel Mold (whom she had raised from his original position as a 'Bodley boy', who foliated manuscripts and fetched books). My portrait is flattering, and Belinda and Nicholas much enjoy rather malicious gossip about their acquaintance (as we did in life), and find pleasure in seeing Henry without the tiresome presence of Agatha.

Agatha was at Karlsbad for her health; there she met a colonial bishop and invited him to visit the vicarage. He turned out to be none other than Theodore Grote, once dearer to Harriet than any other curate; he is now Bishop of Mbawawa. Harriet has to work the magic lantern for his lecture, and Belinda is afraid she will have to lose her sister to darkest Africa; even though to all appearance she dislikes the bishop.

He, ironically, has a bad memory, and remembers Belinda as the Miss Bede who was so kind to him when he was a curate. It is to her that he proposes, and as he is promptly refused the sisters' life is safe.

The book ends without ending, as Barbara's later books were often to do. Readers will better remember how they begin than how they end. The end is often a more or less happy but unimportant occasion – here it is the curate's wedding. There is a comfortable feeling that life will go on in much the same way; there is even a faint atmosphere of optimism – some things may be a little better.

[2]

A Note on *Crampton Hodnet*

Among miscellaneous writings of Barbara Pym's early years there was a completed novel, *Crampton Hodnet*, issued in 1985 by her literary executor. Mrs Holt is mistaken in saying that Barbara sent it to me in 1940, though she may have intended to do so, and that might be on record. I was only in England from 29 February till 3 August in that year. I could not have forgotten the title. Crampton is a Pym family name, Hodnet is the village in Shropshire where the book-collector Richard Heber lived – the whole is the name of an imaginary Cotswold village whose vicar, invented for the occasion, is to provide an alibi for a clergyman who has missed evensong. One otherwise good reviewer mistook it for a 'real' (fictionized) place, and attributed an ethos of its own to it.

This book would hardly have found a publisher but for Barbara's reputation, to which it can do neither harm nor good. There are delightful comic scenes, the best devoted to an attempted love-affair between an Oxford don and an attractive pupil – a chapter of accidents, leaving the don back in his own house silenced by a thermometer stuck in his mouth by his rather dull wife. There is a pleasing nostalgia about the north Oxford atmosphere, and though one does not quite understand those who laughed aloud, few can have read it without many smiles.

It illustrates an early influence upon Barbara's writing. In 1935 (which was late) I first fell under the spell of Ivy Compton-Burnett, and communicated my enthusiasm to Barbara. We wrote imitations of her style, and in letters to each other made every possible occasion into her form of dialogue; my brother also joined in the game. The best example in this book is given by old Mrs Killigrew (whose German origin may connect her with Gretchen Jekyll in *A House and Its Head*).

> 'I have not done good this afternoon. I believe I may have done harm. I must face that. It will be a burden for me to bear, the knowledge that I may have done harm,' she added in a surprisingly light tone.

All through her writing life Barbara made a more or less sparing use of what I have called 'Compton-Burnett stage directions'. She and I were particularly fond of 'a voice drained of all feeling', and many others. Her dialogue is, however, seldom influenced. Another early influence, Stevie Smith's *Novel on Yellow Paper*, is markedly seen in Barbara's letters, but I think only there.

A very good reviewer has found the author's reasons for putting this manuscript aside 'mysterious'. I think, as authors often must, she thought it not good enough to print, but too good to throw away – a useful quarry for material to be used elsewhere. It was later pillaged for *Jane and Prudence*.

Francis Cleveland, an Oxford tutor (*CH*) is writing about the seventeenth-century poet, John Cleveland. The same poet is the subject of Jane Cleveland (*JP*), the vicar's wife.

Barbara Bird appears in *CH* as a very pretty girl in her last year at Oxford (1937), with whom Francis Cleveland is in love. The same name is given to Jane Cleveland's 'college friend', with whom she attended a meeting in 1952. The name is (I think) used in error (or on the assumption that *CH* has been suppressed). The second Barbara Bird is forty-one and the author of seventeen novels, and in no way recalls the first.

Miss Doggett, who is about seventy in 1937 (*CH*), is no older in 1952 (*JP*). She appears to be thoroughly settled in the village, and there is no suggestion that she has moved from north Oxford. Her companion, Jessie Morrow (*CH*), who was a confirmed spinster of thirty-six in 1937, is only one year older in 1952. She is now a successful husband-hunter, but remains the same sardonic personality, and the most interesting character in each of the two books.

After *Jane and Prudence* Barbara could not have intended that *Crampton Hodnet* should ever be published, but no doubt still kept it as a possibly useful quarry.

The distinguished writer* who seeks to compare Barbara Pym's world with that of Jane Austen makes a small slip in telling us that Lady Beddoes in *Clampton Hodnet* 'descends from her little mews-house or flat in Belgravia, where she has taken refuge, to open a church bazaar'. Lady Beddoes is not a refugee of any sort; she is the widow of an ambassador who is thought to have left a considerable fortune. She has a house in Chester Square, and her travels are noted in the social column of newspapers. We are still in the year 1937, and the world of Jane Austen is not yet quite so far away as it will be after the war.

*A.L. Rowse in *The Life and Work of Barbara Pym*, Dale Salwak (ed.), Macmillan, London, 1987, p. 65.

TWO

The 'Canon'

[3]

Introduction to the 'Canon'

A mind lively and at ease can do with seeing nothing, and can see nothing that does not answer.

It is in this respect alone that a comparison may be made between Barbara and Jane Austen – a commonplace with reviewers who, perhaps, do not know Jane Austen's work very well, and remember only that she was a witty and observant writer and preferred to work on a limited canvas.

It is unjust to place any good, talented writer beside Jane Austen, a unique artist, the one poet of the objective or external novel (of course subjective, introspective writers from Laurence Sterne to Virginia Woolf have had their poetry). Elsewhere I have discussed some of her inventions in the art of fiction.* It cannot be called an 'invention' to make Marianne Dashwood (in *Sense and Sensibility*) desperately in love, though no one else in English fiction, save Pip in *Great Expectations*, is quite in this condition. However, the wonderful polyphony of scenes in *Pride and Prejudice* and *Emma*, where the same spoken words heard by different ears have such different meaning, is a device not found in any other writer's work so far as I am aware. Unique also is the lovely trio at Captain Wentworth's proposal in *Persuasion*.

Prose novelists who rightly do not attempt such effects are not

*Robert Liddell, *The Novels of Jane Austen*, Longman, London, 1963.

[27]

to be placed in the same category, though not necessarily in a lower one. Even Ivy Compton-Burnett, who was certainly a writer of genius and who also has added something new to the novel, had in many ways a different mind – her direct verbal influence is sometimes to be noted in Barbara's work, in a conversation or a phrase.

Barbara Pym's great achievement has been to create a world, built up of little things, recognizable (though never repetitive). The Balzacian trick of allowing characters to reappear from book to book (which annoys some readers) adds a further unity to her *oeuvre* already made one by sameness of tone.

The present chapter is concerned with the 'canon', by which I intend the work written before she was unwillingly silenced by the rejection of a novel in 1963. I have considered her first novel by itself, as it represents her beginnings, and the action is set before the war. The 'canon' is a group of high-spirited novels written in more hopeful years before the world was afflicted by inflation, the Churches by 'reforms', and before Barbara herself was attacked by the illness that was to cause her death.

It was these novels that incited Lord David Cecil and Philip Larkin to name her as the most underrated writer of the century in a symposium in *The Times Literary Supplement* in 1977. She was the only living writer to secure two votes. After that her success was assured.

Barbara's world is middle-aged for the most part; about 75 per cent of her characters are aged between thirty and sixty-five. As against Jane Austen's portrait gallery of girls, there are only two sub-heroines, Deirdre (*LA*) and Penelope (*UA*) who are twenty-five or under. No children have speaking parts.

The world is also middle class. Evelyn Waugh has rightly said that every truthful novel about English life must be 'class-conscious' and so are all the books of the 'canon'. That does not mean that books must be snobbish, though some of their characters may be – and snobbery, whose good side may be a love of refinement, is not the dreadful sin that that arch-snob, Proust's

Legrandin, affected to think it. Awareness of differences must be a part of every observant intelligence; some people are obliged by their work to ignore such differences, and we may all have to overlook them from time to time out of kindness, but it can be no part of a novelist's duty. Mildred (*EW*) and Wilmet (*GB*), Barbara's two first-person narrators, must see the world from their own point of view as English gentlewomen of the middle class, safely above the 'Great Divide'. This is the author's own point of view when she uses no narrator – but it is the point of view of someone living at the present day, when differences are not quite the same as they were in the nineteenth century, and life has mixed people more haphazardly together. The novels exhibit a world that is by no means static, even between one book and the next.

'Pymdom', if one may coin the word, is a predominantly Anglo-Catholic country. The church-goers in these books are no doubt genuinely pious (and of this we are sometimes given proof), but theology is not their strong point. The less educated members of the Church are very ignorant of their position. When Mark Ainger (*UA*) says that, as an Anglican, he feels 'almost an intruder' in Rome, Sophia, his wife, rebukes him: 'You who so often preach about the Catholicity of the Anglican Church, and believe it too!' This provokes an ignorant old woman to say: 'Oh, yes, Father... we always say that's one of your little hobby-horses.' This must be the sort of thing to make the clergy feel desperate. And Mildred (*EW*) is probably quite unsuccessful in teaching her Welsh charwoman the nature of the Anglican position.

Of course that position is delicate, and sometimes threatened. 'Poor Mr and Mrs Lake and Miss Spicer' (*EW*) had been received into the Church of Rome, also the 'gentleman' who had been thurifer at Father Lomax's church (*JP*). The question of intercommunion with the Church of South India was troubling many consciences. Marius Ransome (*GB*) was on the verge of 'going over', and his friend Edwin Sainsbury actually did so.

Perhaps it is partly the fear of having to 'go over' as well as an

[29]

atavistic Protestantism that accounts for the fear of nuns and convents entertained even by so thorough an Anglo-Catholic as Wilmet. Whereas people like Jane, married to a moderately Low Church clergyman, hanker after High Church ritual and 'solemn evensong and benediction'.

Curates may be turned into comic characters by excessive feminine devotion (*STG*) but beneficed clergy are seriously treated and as individualized as anyone else, unless they occur merely as names, such as Father Tulliver (*LA*). Wilmet's mother-in-law Sybil (*GB*) went to a play where the audience 'roared with laughter when the vicar entered through the French windows at the back of the stage' – evidently the 'comic parson' of *The Private Secretary* still survived in the theatre. Wilmet disapproved of such disrespectful treatment of the clergy, and so no doubt did Barbara. Of course there are reviewers who have spoken of someone as a 'typically Barbara Pym' clergyman – there is no such person. Her clergy include serious, manly priests who do their duty and rather dislike it, such as Mark Ainger, Julian Malory, Nicholas Cleveland – sometimes they are married, sometimes they 'tend towards celibacy', and this may expose them to the pursuit of 'church workers'. Thus Father Neville Forbes (*NFR*) has to take refuge with his mother. One of them, the Archdeacon, is a great eccentric; another, Father Thames, is a gourmet and a connoisseur of *objets de vertù* with one foot in Italy; while his assistant, Father Bode, is a common, pious little man, full of practical charity. The clergy, however, are but men, and like ordinary laymen are only too much inclined to shift their 'burdens' – of which they often speak – on to the shoulders of women, the stronger sex.

Barbara's women will have to be considered one by one, but some generalization at this stage may be useful.

She and her heroines would not have agreed with Donne:

> Whoever loves, if he do not propose
> The right true end of love, he's one that goes
> To sea for nothing but to make him sick.

[30]

They are absorbed by the minor pleasures of love: the satisfaction of always having something to think about, of never feeling bored in a waiting-room or needing a book or paper.

The 'canon' was composed before *Lady Chatterley* was acquitted, to the detriment of subsequent fiction.* In the 'canon' love is never made and no 'nasty' word is uttered. Even in the later books there is only one hurried and casual copulation, and one four-letter word.

The love-stories are always muted; love is unrequited, or directed to an unsuitable object. In fact (though this object is not 'strange' or 'high')

It is begotten by despair upon impossibility.

That is, as often as not. Jane Austen always unites at least one pair of lovers at the end of every novel, and leaves them with good prospects of future happiness. Barbara only publicly unites not very important characters; the two weddings (*STG* and *UA*) are mainly useful as farewell receptions for the other people in the book. Sometimes people who meet during the course of a novel marry between this one and the next, in which their marriage is baldly reported, though it seems likely to be happy.

Certainly, men being what they are, the heroines have not much to choose from. Jane Austen's world was richer; anyone would confidently entrust a daughter or a sister to a landowner like Darcy or George Knightley, a clergyman like Edward Ferrars, Edmund Bertram or Henry Tilney, or to an officer like Colonel Brandon or Captain Wentworth. Perhaps it should be remembered that Jane Austen had five brothers to whom she was much attached and whom she probably thought too good for their wives.

It is rare that Pym women are the object of pursuit, nearly every one of them is a huntress – but one feels that they hunt for sport (so to speak) not for food. They are all eager emotionally for love, but

*"'Physical consummation means fictional flatness,' John Bayley in *The Life and Work of Barbara Pym*, p. 57.

on the whole they seem not to like the idea of sex. I leave to other pens all speculations about the connection between her works and Barbara's own psyche as revealed in her diaries. I expect someone will say that a happy marriage might have solved what looks like a dichotomy – it might be so, but it could have killed her as a writer. It is perhaps significant that in the case of many good women writers marriage has preceded publication – as it precedes ordination in the case of orthodox clergy. One thinks of Mrs Humphry Ward, Mrs Henry de la Pasture, Mrs Woolf and Mrs Taylor.

> All is best, though we oft doubt,
> What th' unsearchable dispose
> Of highest wisdom brings about. . . .

I think Barbara would agree, 'though in many ways one dislikes Milton, of course; his treatment of women was not all that it should have been'. I shall confine myself to contradicting the reviewer (otherwise perceptive) who denied that she had a heart.

In any case the world has changed not only since the time of Jane Austen but also since the period in which the action of Ivy Compton-Burnett's novels is situated. Then the only profession open to an unmarried gentlewoman was teaching, in a school or as a governess, unless she became a rich woman's 'companion'. Now even a rich débutante could say that '*everyone* did something nowadays' (*LA*). Emma, at the age of twenty-one, could (as she was an heiress) afford to look forward to spinsterdom, for 'a single woman of good fortune is always respectable, and may be as sensible and pleasant as anybody else'. The only successful husband-hunter in the 'canon' is impelled by the resolve not to end up as a 'distressed gentlewoman'. The other women have some private means, or are able to earn a competence.

The changes in post-war life put heavier burdens upon the 'excellent women' of the Pym world than on anyone else – indeed a man whose 'womenfolk' were particularly excellent must have felt them comparatively little. The novels of the 'canon' more than any others of the time show how a large section of the community actually *lived* – and one day they will have an historical as well as a literary interest.

Dr Johnson wrote to his friend Baretti what might be an 'apology' for such writing.

> I will not trouble you with speculations about peace and war. The good or ill success of battles and embassies extends to a very small part of domestic life: we all have good and evil, which we feel more sensibly than our petty part of publick miscarriage or prosperity.

'Publick miscarriage' had caused the changes in 'domestick life' – but we are here invited to examine the effects and not the cause. The immediate effects were the difficulties of obtaining the food one needed or desired; the more lasting (and worsening) effects were the disappearance of domestic service.

The characters in *Some Tame Gazelle* lived comfortably before the Second World War, looked after by resident servants. Agatha, who was stingy, kept a very poor table at the vicarage, but the Bedes' table was well covered and, on occasion, 'groaning'. Chickens (as illiterate authors of cookery books would express it) were 'embalmed' with sauce, and trifles 'shrouded' with cream – and that was not all.

In *Excellent Women* the lean years have come. Mildred has her 'woman', Mrs Morris, who comes twice a week to clean her flat, and the Malorys at the Vicarage have Mrs Jubb to do their dreary cooking. Jane (*JP*) has a treasure in Mrs Glaze, who does the cooking when Jane's daughter is away, and some of the housework – but we do not hear of anyone in *Less than Angels*, except the rich and retired scholar Felix, who has any sort of domestic help. He has a man-servant and a cook, and employs an awkward girl from the village to wait at table when he has guests. Wilmet and her mother-in-law have an invaluable Rhoda down in their basement, who can make a perfect cheese soufflé (*GB*). Her friend Rowena has her nails 'uncared for, hardly even clean', though 'she had a reasonable amount of domestic help' and an Italian au pair girl to look after the children. Dulcie (*NFR*) is lucky in her Miss Lord, who will come in for extra hours at need. Rupert Stonebird (*UA*) was well cooked for by his 'daily woman', Mrs Purry. In short the Pym world was less uncomfortable than it well might be, but most people did their own cooking, and all of the women did a great deal of washing-up.

Food was more difficult. Soon after the war scrambled eggs in a tea-room would not be 'real'. 'Curried whale' could be offered on a menu, and an unwary Anglo-Catholic might eat it on a Friday, not realizing that the whale is a mammal and cannot count as fish. People decorating a room, and directed to mix their paint to the colour of cream, cannot remember what cream was like. One hesitates to accept a spoonful from another person's jam ration. We are 'told not to waste bread'. Who tells us? 'They', no doubt – indistinctly imagined beings like those of Edward Lear, some sort of killjoy authority like Sir Stafford Cripps. The cooking of a small joint is such a rare occasion that it is charged with emotion (*EW*).

Jane Cleveland (*JP*) is the wife of a vicar just settling down in a country parish. Mrs Glaze, who 'does' for her, brings her some liver, saying 'Meat has never been at such a low ebb as it is now, what with everything having to go through the Government; it's no wonder the butchers can't go on grinding out the ration isn't it, madam?' Her nephew the butcher 'shares out the [unrationed] offal on a fair basis'. Those who do not get it this time will get it next. The local eligible widower, Fabian Driver, will probably have a 'casserole of hearts' for his lunch, cooked by Mrs Arkwright who 'does' for him – appropriately, as he has the reputation of a lady-killer.

It is difficult to make do on the rations. Jane, as many housewives did at that time, finds it necessary to send her husband out to luncheon at least twice a week. Nicholas Cleveland, the vicar, in masculine ignorance, thinks they might have stayed at home and opened a tin of Spam. He did not realize that there was no Spam any more; it had come from America during the war. So Jane and he visited the Spinning Wheel, one of those admirable little tea-shops once frequently run by ladies. They are given eggs (two for the vicar and one for his wife) and bacon by Mrs Crampton and Mrs Mayhew. Most people in the village would have gone early to the butcher's for sausages, and now would be eating 'toad-in-the-hole' – a dish for which Barbara seems to have had a particular abhorrence, for 'toad' recurs rather too often in the novels. Eggs are now a little less difficult to obtain. Throughout the 'canon', the men are intensely and unreflectively selfish, and spoilt by the women. 'A man needs meat,' says Mrs Crampton (or Mrs Mayhew – *because both meant, both spake the same*) and however short it is in supply, he gets it.

In *Less than Angels* the lean years are more or less over; you can buy a real calf's foot from the butcher for *boeuf à la mode*. Catherine, the heroine, seems always to find scraps of meat to offer up to her mincing-machine Beatrice, 'a strangely gentle and gracious name for the fierce little iron contraption whose strong teeth so ruthlessly pounded up meat and gristle'. It always reminded Catherine of an African god 'with its square head and little short arms' – appropriately it supplied her with the wherewithal for risotti for anthropologist visitors. The second heroine, Deirdre, has a mother and aunt who are fond of giving supper parties – and though a 'bird' is the most suitable dish to offer to a clergyman (as the Misses Bede thought in *STG*), the anthropologists also invited will have eaten chicken too often in Africa, and other meat must be provided – this seems to present no difficulty. The two learned ladies, Gertrude Lydgate and Esther Clovis, 'live out of tins and on frozen stuff', and always choose 'the kind of meat you can fry – chops and things like that'. They seem to have no difficulty in getting them.

Cafeterias and restaurants of different classes are much used, especially by working characters at lunch-time; no character in the novels of Jane Austen or Ivy Compton-Burnett ever ate in a restaurant or alone. These have not the topicality of food eaten at home: the baked beans of the cheaper places are timeless, though the beautiful sirloin rolled up on a trolley at Simpson's could not have been there in the years of austerity. There is a dreadful sense of eternity about the dinner, served at 6.45 p.m. at the Anchorage (*NFR*), a private hotel which advertises its 'bright Christian atmosphere'.

An outside observer of English life was a young French anthropologist, Jean Pierre le Rossignol. He went to Father Tulliver's church (*LA*) to observe suburban life on a Sunday, and remained to lunch with Deirdre's family.

The aunt says, of her sister:

> 'She is at home cooking the meal – of course things are not as they were,' she added obscurely.
>
> Deirdre supposed that she must be remembering the old days when they would have had a cook.
>
> 'There has been quite a social revolution in England I believe,' said Jean-Pierre politely. 'The dynamics of culture change.'
>
> 'Such a pity,' said Rhoda, puzzling over the end of his sentence. 'In some ways, that is. Of course one *does* want things to be shared more equally, that is good...'
>
> 'Provided one gets the larger share oneself,' said Jean-Pierre....

And unfortunately it will be the mother and the aunt who have to do the washing-up.

Always there is a faint, ungrudging nostalgia for 'better days' in the past, concealed by many of Barbara's characters with a hypocrisy which is theirs ('things are better now') and never her own, for she often provides a corrective.

A good example is the scene (*UA*) where Mark Ainger, the vicar, and Sophia, his wife, call on a single woman, Ianthe Broome, lately settled in the parish.

[36]

'Those were painted by my grandmother,' said Ianthe, seeing that Sophia was examining the water-colours of Italian scenes which hung in the hall. 'People seemed to stay abroad so much longer in those days and have time to do things like that.'

'Yes, they were leisured days,' said Mark, a little uncomfortably, feeling that he should say that things were 'better' now when great coachloads of people could whirl round the Italian lakes in an eight-day tour. But he found himself unable to say it, especially not to this very obvious gentlewoman.

Publishers at one time told Barbara that people were not 'turning' to her sort of book. They seem to have been mistaken as, when she was rediscovered, people turned to her books in thousands. I see her success as the triumph of the Common Reader, bored with the contemporary novel such as that (*PJ*) which 'described a love affair in the fullest sense of the word and sparing no detail', or those burdened with politics or 'social messages' which would better have been conveyed in non-fiction works. No doubt some reviewers would use the out-of-date word 'escapism'. Certainly the mild comedy of Pymdom does not pose such penetrating questions for self-examination as do the works of Jane Austen or Ivy Compton-Burnett; and Barbara, who has caused some laughter and many smiles, has made no one shed a tear. Nevertheless, an occasional retreat from an uglier world into books concerned with constant elements in human nature must be bracing, and not relaxing. And, alas, the 1950s which they depict can now be felt in some ways as 'better days'. In a worsening world we may at any moment give a new and cruel meaning to Aeneas' words: *forsan et haec olim meminisse iuvabit*. Our own days may in memory come to be seen as 'better days'.

[4]

The Kitchen Sink

Excellent Women, a novel of the very lean years, shows the Pym woman at the lowest ebb of her experience and expectations. It is, I think, the best novel in the 'canon'.

There are two synchronous stories, one of the Church, the other of the world; in consequence there is more of a plot than elsewhere in the 'canon', and since so much of the author's thought is inseparable from the people and the happenings, some account of the story must be given.

The single, first-person narrator is Mildred Lathbury, a most excellent woman. She tells us what she knows and what she feels, and we never get ahead of her. 'I suppose an unmarried woman just over thirty, who lives alone and has no apparent ties, must expect to find herself involved or interested in other people's business, and if she is a clergyman's daughter then one might really say there is no hope for her.'

Underlying her stories of other people is her own story of dislike for a man turning to sympathy and friendship and (almost) to love. This probably needed time to come about. Mildred had missed 'not only the experience of marriage, but the perhaps greater and more ennobling one of having loved and lost'; while Everard might have 'an attraction for the kind of person who is drawn to the unusual even the unpleasant'. In the next novel (*JP*) we are not surprised to learn that they have married. It was wise to give no date for this.

[38]

If any student, wishing to be original, attempts to impugn Mildred's straightforwardness and to turn her into that favourite 'thesis' character, the false narrator – responsible, for example, for the flight of Helena Napier or the debasement of Allegra Gray – he will look even more foolish than those who attack Nelly Dean in *Wuthering Heights*, and will not have the success of those who still malign the governess in *The Turn of the Screw*.* He will probably have his reward, a PhD.

Mildred provides the setting:

> I sometimes thought how strange it was that I should have managed to make a life for myself in London so very much like the life I had lived in a country rectory when my parents were alive. But then so many parts of London have a peculiarly village or parochial atmosphere that perhaps it is only a question of choosing one's parish and fitting into it.

The atmosphere emanating from 'St Mary's, Pimlico' (of which the original was St Gabriel's, Warwick Square) turns the parish into a more coherent village than that which we shall meet in the next book (*JP*).

Mildred has a fairly roomy flat, though she has to share a bathroom with the flat below. '"I have to share a bathroom," I had so often murmured, almost with shame, as if I personally had been found unworthy of a bathroom of my own.' This is one of the author's rare 'girlishisms' – which we may compare with one or two in *Pride and Prejudice*.† She has inherited some private means and some good furniture but (unlike a Jane Austen heroine) she seems to have no family connections. She does part-time work for a society for distressed gentlewomen. She usually leaves her flat at a quarter to nine every morning and works for her gentlewomen till lunch-time – but sometimes she is at home at eleven o'clock

---

*I suspect a secret envy of goodness is behind these and similar theories.
†See Robert Liddell, *The Novels of Jane Austen*, pp. 40–41.

when her cleaning woman, Mrs Morris (who comes two mornings a week), says, 'Kettle's boiling, Miss', and they have tea.

At the beginning of the book her main social life was with the vicar, Father Julian Malory, and Winifred his sister. She is a complete illustration of Keble's lines:

> The trivial round, the common task
> Will furnish all we need to ask.

They will furnish not only enough for sanctification, but would provide enough for an entertaining novel, even if there were nothing else. Mildred finds that 'practically anything may be the business of an unattached woman with no troubles of her own, who takes a kindly interest in those of her friends'. She is constantly making tea for the Church world, but there are more exacting tasks. Already at home she has learned how to cope with the greater events: 'Birth, marriage, death, the successful jumble sale, the garden fête spoilt by bad weather.' Church tasks are unending: things must be sorted for the jumble sale (photographs tactfully removed from their frames); the day must be fixed, the stall-holders appointed, and the toughest acolytes conscripted to keep back the rough crowd who will rush in to buy. The church must be decorated for festivals – Mildred is humbly responsible for putting a small bunch of pinks into a potted meat jar, wired to the rood screen.

Often she eats a white and tasteless meal with the vicar and his sister. She has been thought of as a suitable wife for the vicar by everyone else except herself and him. Julian is by no means the kind of clergyman who could ever have been a favourite curate. 'There was usually something rather forbidding in his manner so that women did not tend to fuss over him as they might otherwise have done. I am not sure whether anyone had ever knitted him a scarf or a pullover.' He had not definitely resolved on celibacy, but it was convenient for his sister to live with him, 'and perhaps it is more suitable that a High Church clergyman should remain

[40]

unmarried, that there should be a biretta in the hall rather than a perambulator'.

When Julian lets the upper floor of the vicarage, Mildred is called upon to help with distempering the walls, and even arranging what the tenant, Allegra Gray, is to pay. She must also help to adapt Mrs Gray's curtains.

The vicar falls a victim to the charms of his tenant, a clergyman's widow with an apricot complexion. There are two delightful scenes when the engagement is broken to Mildred. Allegra asks her to luncheon and, it seemed 'She was trying to tell me how glad and relieved she was that I didn't mind too much when I must surely have wanted to marry Julian myself.' Julian is more awkward: 'Dear Mildred, it would have been a fine thing if it could have been' (that is, a marriage between them, which he cannot believe she never wanted). Such completely original scenes (as I believe these to be) prove the vitality of the novel, so often thrown in doubt.

The engagement breaks down because Allegra is determined to get Winifred out of the house. Everyone now expects Julian to turn to Mildred, and he seems to think of it, but she does not encourage him.

The episode is self-contained, though its scenes alternate with that by which Mildred is to be more personally affected, the story of the couple in the flat underneath her own.

Mildred has no real difficulty in managing her two parallel lives, with people of the Church and people of the world.

Some critics seem to take peculiar pleasure in Barbara's occasional jests at 'organized religion' as if they meant more than they do. She was no 'exception to the rule that enthusiasm for religious subjects is coupled with a tendency to pleasantry upon them'.* And pleasantry is most apt to be directed towards the little humours of 'organized religion' such as the heating apparatus in the church, the bazaar, the absurdity of many hymns, or the

---

*Ivy Compton-Burnett, *Dolores*, Blackwoods, London, 1911, 2nd edn 1971.

unpleasantness* that arises when Mildred's friend Dora allows her form to attend the school chapel without wearing hats.

Mildred, of course, would not care whether the girls wore hats or not; but she would not applaud Dora's breach of a school rule as a piece of progressive defiance of a superstitious practice; it was simply bad-mannered neglect of the headmistress's wishes, not disrespect to St Paul.

Barbara would probably suspect that those who spoke contemptuously of 'organized religion' were most often entirely irreligious, for spirituality and a sacramental life require an organized framework. Moreover she allows Mildred to show great contempt for 'disorganized religion', if one may apply the phrase to 'talking about it being just as easy to worship God in a beechwood or on the golf links on a fine Sunday morning'.

Julian Malory is an energetic, manly priest in a poor parish: hardly ever does he make a pietistic remark or drop into clerical speech, though he never conceals the fact that he must take a different stand from that taken by Mildred's lay friends, in particular about marriage. He is deservedly respected, and can even help in difficult personal situations as he could not, if he compromised. Mildred is rather embarrassed at his suggestions that she should take every opportunity of 'saying a word' on the right side when she is confronted with unbelievers, and she knows how ineffective and awkward it would probably prove. Nevertheless the convinced Christianity of Julian and Mildred, and that of Everard Bone later revealed to us, does leaven the whole book. Mildred feels as if all clergymen are her personal responsibility:

*This is the term used by William, a minor character, superfluous in an analysis of this book – though he turns up from time to time throughout the 'canon' – who is the brother of Mildred's school friend Dora: he takes Mildred out to luncheon rarely but regularly. I like to think I am William, or perhaps have merely contributed to him – for I am not a bird-lover nor a connoisseur of wine, and Barbara and I had other friends inclined to be snobbish and greedy, and addicted to malicious conversation – we liked people like that. When she visited Oxford I used to take her to dinner at a restaurant where, at least, she could see 'the young barbarians all at meat'. No doubt William could feed her better in Soho. The Oxford restaurant 'shrouded' (the funereal word is fitting) nearly everything in a concoction in which Worcester sauce and curry powder dominated.

'and perhaps they were when I was up against unbelievers'.

The book opens with the arrival of the newcomers to Mildred's building – a favourite beginning for a novel from Jane Austen onwards: the entry of new people on the scene. They are Rockingham Napier,* a naval officer who has been a flag lieutenant in Italy, adored by all the Wren officers, and Helena his wife, an anthropologist who has been working in Africa with another scholar, Everard Bone.

Mildred frequently makes coffee, and tea too, for this more sophisticated world, and though her 'woman', Mrs Morris, also 'does' for the Napiers, it is not enough. Mildred finds herself cleaning up the mess that the sluttish Helena leaves in her flat, empties ashtrays, and scrapes burnt saucepans. We see her at the kitchen sink, so dominant in the art of that period.

> No sink has ever been built high enough for a reasonably tall person and my back was soon aching with the effort of washing up, especially as yesterday's greasy dishes needed a lot of scrubbing to get them clean. My thoughts went round and round, and it occurred to me that if I ever wrote a novel it would be of the stream of consciousness type and deal with an hour in the life of a woman at the sink.

That Mildred could write a novel we cannot doubt. Her grisly picture of the 'ladies' room' in a large store is something like an Alma Tadema in modern dress, with a touch of Goya.

> Inside it was a sobering sight indeed, and one to put us all in the mind of the futility of material things and of our own mortality.

*Rockingham had once been used by Barbara in an unpublished fragment, more appropriately, as the first name of a clergyman. For I do not think that it came from the china, though Mrs Beltane (NFR) had Rockingham fruit plates. I think it came from the tune usually sung to Dr Watts's noble hymn, 'When I Survey the Wondrous Cross'.

I recollect that in the fragment the clergyman's wife told him, quite truthfully, that a Hungarian had settled in their village. 'Ask yourself, my dear,' said Rockingham incredulously, 'why a Hungarian should settle here.'

All flesh is grass ... I thought, watching the women working at their faces with strange concentration, biting and licking their lips, stabbing at their noses and chins with powder-puffs. Some had abandoned the struggle to keep up, sat in chairs, their bodies slumped down, their hands resting on their parcels. One woman lay on a couch, her hat and shoes off, her eyes closed I tiptoed past her with my penny in my hand.

Some readers have complained that the book begins too slowly; they ask for more than 'the trivial round, the common task'. Others will accept that 'Life was like that for most of us – the small unpleasantnesses rather than the great tragedies, the little useless longings rather than the great renunciations and dramatic love affairs of history and fiction.'

'The little useless longings' soon manifest themselves. Rocky is good-looking – but so are Aylwin and Neville Forbes (*NFR*) and other male characters whose good looks mean little to us – it is always difficult for an author to remember that the reader is *blind*, and that no one has movingly described a face. But Rocky has also charm, which can be conveyed to the reader; perhaps Father Marius Ransome is the only other man in the 'canon' of whom this can be predicated. We hear (from a former Wren) that she and her sister-officers suffered temporary infatuations for him, lasting normally not more than six weeks. But if he was kind he was also shallow and vain, and had an Italian mistress. Mildred is half in love with him, as Helena amusedly points out to her – but she disciplines herself by picturing the awkward Wren officers in their ill-fitting uniforms and by remembering the Italian mistress. Anyway, as she says righteously to Julian Malory, Rocky is a married man.

Helena is worse placed. She has fallen in love with Everard Bone, with whom she had been working in 'the field', and they are preparing a paper to be read to a learned society. Rocky is entirely uninterested in their anthropological research.

Everard, however, is not in the least in love with Helena. Moreover he is a good churchman, converted while at Cambridge.

Mildred is surprised to see him at a Lenten lunch-time service in the surviving aisle of bombed St Ermin's (which I fancy is St Peter's, Eaton Square): and her first feeling of sympathy for him is aroused by finding that he too is amused by a sermon from our old friend Archdeacon Hoccleve (STG). Of course Everard will be opposed to the remarriage of divorced persons, and Mildred has wronged him in thinking that he wants to break up the Napiers' marriage.

She has made a Lenten resolution to like him better, and when he reads his paper she tries to study him, to find out what Helena sees in him.

> He was certainly very clever and handsome, too, in his own way, but there was no warmth or charm about his personality, I began imagining him as a clergyman and decided that he would make a good one. His rather forbidding manner would be useful to him. I realised that one might love him secretly with no hope of encouragement, which can be very enjoyable for the young and inexperienced.

In short, he had much in common with Julian Malory.

Oddly enough, when Mildred was tidying her flat, she came across a large photograph of the young man with whom she had once imagined herself in love – and there had been no other. Bernard was a bank clerk, who had occasionally read the lessons at her father's church; Flora Cleveland (JP) was to fall in love with such another. It came to nothing, but Mildred had embarrassed recollections of hurrying past his lodgings in the dusk. Now his face reminded her a little of Everard Bone.

Not long afterwards she found Everard waiting outside her office. She was carrying a string bag with a loaf of bread and a biography of Cardinal Newman. He complained that Helena had been behaving in a most foolish and indiscreet way. She had come to his flat one night and had stayed for nearly three hours talking. 'You could perhaps say something to Helena,' he said – but when

[45]

she passed their door on the way to her flat Mildred heard the Napiers' voices raised in argument.

Next day it was too late; Helena had gone. A gas ring was on, and on it

a saucepan of potatoes which had boiled dry and were now sticking to the bottom in a brownish mess ... the breakfast things and what appeared to be dishes and glasses from an even earlier date were not washed up. The table by the window was also crowded; there were two bottles of milk, each half full, an empty gin bottle, a dish of butter melting in the sun, and a plate full of cigarette stubs.

A hot saucepan had been put down on a polished walnut table, and that had been 'the last straw', for Rocky cared for his furniture.

Mildred took Rocky up to her flat to have some lunch. He suggested that Helena had gone to Everard Bone – 'the irrelevant and unworthy thought crossed my mind that he would think I had failed in my duty.... But I had really had very little time in which to tell Helena that Everard did not love her.'

She rang him up, but Everard said in alarm that Helena had not come and that he was leaving at once for a conference of the Prehistoric Society in Derbyshire. And, of course, Mildred went downstairs to clear up the Napiers' mess.

Helena took refuge with Esther Clovis, on the staff of the Learned Society. Rocky directed what furniture and objects were to be sent to his country cottage, and went away – leaving Mildred in shock and grief. Miss Clovis hoped Helena would now be free to give all her thought to anthropology: 'You will now be able to devote your whole life to the study of matrilineal kin-groups.' Ironically, Helena goes instead to her mother in Devonshire.

Everard some time later waylays Mildred on a sudden impulse, and is much relieved by the news she gives him of the Napiers. He says he would not have married Helena even if she had been free, but a 'sensible woman'. 'Excellent women', says Mildred, 'are for being unmarried ... and by that I mean a positive rather than a negative state.'

Shortly afterwards three things happen. Julian breaks his engagement, the Napiers are reconciled – and between these contrasting events Everard telephones Mildred and asks her to come to dinner and help him to cook a small joint, but she excuses herself. 'He would be quite equal to cooking a joint. Men are not nearly so helpless and pathetic as we sometimes like to imagine them, and on the whole they run their lives better than we do ours.' How did she know that she was the first person that Everard had asked? She felt disturbed and no longer in the mood to enjoy a quiet evening at home.

Next time it was she who contrived a meeting in the street, and Everard took her out to luncheon and invited her to dine at his flat another day. Mildred went, expecting to find Esther Clovis there, that paragon of a 'sensible woman', correcting proofs or making an index, and she determined to look like a person who could do no such things. In vain. There was no other guest, and in the warmth of after-dinner coffee Everard was asking her to correct a bundle of proofs. 'Reading proofs for a long stretch gets a little boring. The index would make a nice change for you.' Only a Pym man could make such a suggestion.

Mildred gives way, and we are not surprised to hear in the next novel (*JP*) that she and Everard are married. It is a skilful, muted story, convincing at each stage – and the small joint, whatever its weight, seems to have turned the scale.

From later novels we hear that Mildred is useful when they are 'in the field'; as a clergyman's daughter she gets on well with missionaries. At home her typewriter is at the service of anthropology (*LA*). It seems to be a happy marriage, yet we almost feel that Mildred has betrayed her vocation as an 'excellent woman' – like a nun returning to the world. We could probably accept her as a married woman if we were asked to meet her, but it is well we do not have to witness courtship or the marriage ceremony.

The Village and the Office

Jane and Prudence is a slighter book with a single story, for Jane is a comfortably married woman for whom 'stories' are over.

Jane Cleveland, aged forty-one, is a clergy wife. 'Three times a Sunday they have to be sitting there [in church] in their dowdy old clothes in a pew rather too near the front – it's a kind of duty'. Jane had meant to be 'such a splendid clergyman's wife ... but somehow it hadn't turned out like *The Daisy Chain* or *The Last Chronicle of Barset*'. She is quite unlike Mildred the careful housewife and Helena the slut. She tries hard, but she simply has no notion of order or comfort and is entirely inefficient and somewhat harum-scarum in her appearance. She will wear an old tweed coat fit only for feeding the chickens in, and with it a good new hat bought for a recent wedding. Her general conversation, though educated, is as haphazard as her use of quotations. For example, a bank clerk comes to tea: 'I always think of the mediaeval, banking houses in Florence,' she says, 'great times those must have been.'

Jane had been a temporary tutor in English literature at her Oxford college. She had once published a small critical volume, and had even planned a monograph on her husband's namesake, the poet John Cleveland. Her head is full of verse and a 'not quite appropriate quotation would come into her mind on nearly every occasion' – and it would often come out, too.

By Jane's exuberance in English poetry, Barbara makes up for her self-denial in this book as regards to her two other favourite themes, church and anthropology. Nicholas Cleveland, if not positively Low Church, is Moderate, certainly not High – there is not much to be made of that, and he is without a curate. During his absence on holiday the *locum tenens*, Mr Boultbee of the Missionary Society, so thoroughly bored the parish with sermons about Africa that perhaps the author is careful not to do the same.

She makes, however, an odd slip in attributing to Jane a comparison from anthropology which, though just in itself, is one most unlikely for Jane to make. Prudence has been preparing for a whist drive, at which she hoped to meet eligible men, and her eyelids were 'startlingly and embarrassingly green, glistening with some greasy preparation which had little flecks of silver in it – what hard work it must be, always remembering to add these little touches; there was something primitive about it, like the young African smearing himself with red cam-wood before he went courting'. One would rather expect Jane to be in the position of the character who confused anthropologists with anthropophagists – she could not have heard of red cam-wood.

There came a day when one didn't quote poetry to one's husband any longer. When had that day been? Could she have noted it and mourned it if she had been more observant?

> 'What doth my she-advowson fly
> Incumbency?'

she murmured. Unsuitable of course, but she loved the lines.

Jane need not have worried, such a day would never come to her.

She has great charm and no tact, and can be infuriating to live with; the parishioners do not think much of her. She is said to resemble Barbara's mother, and many of us have been lucky enough to know and love, and to lose all patience with people like her. She has perhaps never thought of herself as a gentlewoman, but she could not exist in any other class.

Prudence Bates (aged twenty-nine), so the author has told us, was one of her favourite characters. At moments, I suspect, Barbara wished to be more like her, and feared to be more like Mildred. Prudence, like Harriet (*STG*), needed *something to love*, but was very catholic in her choice. She had been Jane's pupil at Oxford, and remained her friend. At Oxford she had had many admirers, 'Laurence and Henry and Philip, so many of them', but for some time now 'she had got into the way of preferring unsatisfactory love-affairs to any others, so that it was almost becoming a bad habit'. She works at a 'vague cultural organization', which is perhaps a little too vague as her boss, Arthur Grampian, is somewhere else spoken of as an economist. She shares a room there with two other women, Miss Trapnell and Miss Clothier, who are some years away from either youth or retirement. 'There existed between them a kind of neutral relationship and they banded together against the inconsiderateness of their employer and the follies and carelessness of the two young typists.' Their main interest seems to be in the exact fulfilment of their hours of work: Prudence (whose status is indefinite but slightly higher) will occasionally take small liberties about this. There is also a 'kind of research assistant', a young man, Geoffrey Manifold, who has a room to himself and 'keeps to his own mysterious business'. 'If one were asked point-blank it would really be difficult to say what any of them, even Dr Grampian, actually did; perhaps the young typists' duties were the most clearly defined, for it was certain that they made tea, took shorthand and typed letters which did not always make sense.' Dr Grampian seems to enjoy an apparently undeserved prestige in the learned world, and Prudence, for want of anyone better, cherishes a devotion to him of which he is quite unaware, and she finds the 'lack of *rapport*' hurtful. One can hardly wonder that Jane does not take this seriously, for the reader cannot either.

The office atmosphere is too negative; the author was evidently not much interested in it, and may have feared to bore her readers. This is a not infrequent happening; it is not surprising that such a small proportion of fictional characters do regular work, such work being often so dull. Prudence in the office is almost 'of the first Nothing the Elixir grown'; it is ironical that Jane, the dowdy clergy wife, brings her to life.

Prudence and Jane visit each other. Prudence goes down for weekends in the country, braving the cold vicarage. Jane goes up to London to buy books for confirmation candidates, facing the misery of the train journey: 'the tea too weak or too strong, the stale sandwich, the grimy upholstery, the window that won't open, the waiting on the draughty platform' – and then arrival at Prudence's spiky, uncomfortable Regency flat.

In contrast with Prudence's office, there is 'such richness' of humanity in Jane's village. Here class differences are more closely defined than in London and there is more variety. Edward Lyall, 'our dear member' of Parliament, a charming, shy young man, and his mother, are members of an old county family. The educated middle class is represented by Nicholas and Jane Cleveland, by the formidable old Miss Doggett and Jessie Morrow her sardonic companion (who have been sketched in *Crampton Hodnet*), and by Mrs Crampton and Mrs Mayhew, the proprietors of the tea-room, the Spinning-Wheel.

The broken-hearted widower, Fabian Driver, is very handsome, but just a thought common. Barbara seems to have felt a faint hesitation about telling us this, as a writer of an earlier generation might have felt some inhibition in telling us of his sexual irregularities, Without more than a few hints she lets him go out for a country walk with an umbrella – and we know what Nancy Mitford would have said to that. Now, looking back, we think that his late wife Constance (a few years his senior) must have married beneath her. We know that the money had been hers, and that Fabian had inherited a business from her father – which sometimes took him up to London on ploys as indeterminate as Dr Grampian's. We have only to look at Constance's shoes: 'long and narrow and of such good leather', a gentlewoman's shoes. Jessie, though in love with Fabian and intending to marry him, uncharitably imagined him as wearing brown-and-white shoes.

Of course Francis Oliver, the bank clerk, whose suit was 'too bright blue to be the thing', is certainly not a gentleman; he has only to open his mouth to give himself away. Jane's daughter, Flora, tells him she is going up to Oxford.

'Ah, to study. What subject, may I ask?' he says. He need say no more.

One may wonder with what accent he used to read the lessons in Nicholas's church. He will do better with a thurible at the High Church in the next village, to which he transfers his allegiance.

If there are people who are irritated by such trifles (and I am sure there are) they are not suitable readers for Barbara Pym. Other pens may dwell on the differences between the conservative MP Edward Lyall and his vaguely left-wing mother; here we are more interested in Fabian Driver's chances of being elected to the parochial church council.

Constance had died about a year before the beginning of the book. 'Her death came as a great shock to him – he had almost forgotten her existence', so Jessie tells Jane, who had been surprised to see a large framed photograph of the widower on Constance's grave instead of a stone. Fabian was now 'fancying himself more in the rôle of an inconsolable widower than as a lover. Indeed it was now almost a year since he had thought of anybody but himself. But now he felt that he might start again.'

Jane's plan of marrying him to Prudence seems promising. Their acquaintance, begun at the whist drive, prospered. She was good-looking and elegant; he liked taking her to dine in good restaurants in London, after a discreet drink at her flat; and she was indulgent about his lack of conversation, being able to provide enough herself. Jane looks forward to having her as a neighbour, and Miss Doggett thinks a young and attractive woman like Prudence may keep Fabian out of mischief.

'Men are very passionate,' declared Miss Doggett.

'You mean that they only want one thing?' said Jane.
'Well, yes, that is it. We know what it is.'

'Typing a man's thesis, correcting proofs, putting sheets sides-to-middle, bringing up children, balancing the house-keeping budget – all these are nothing, really,' said Jane in a sad, thoughtful tone.

But men require flattery too.

Oh, but it was splendid the things women were doing for men all the time, thought Jane. Making them feel, perhaps, sometimes by no more than a casual glance that they were loved and admired and desired when they were worthy of none of these things – enabling them to preen themselves and puff out their plumage like birds and bask in the sunshine of love, real or imagined, it didn't matter which.

As always, in the 'canon', all the men are selfish, and spoilt by the women; they all groan under their 'burdens', but it is generally the women who have to bear the heavier part. Even Nicholas says: 'Tea not ready yet?' ... 'in the way men do, not pausing to consider that some woman may at that very moment be pouring the water into the pot'. Jane tries to share his burdens, but it must be admitted that she makes some of them more tiresome by her tactlessness. There is keen competition to share 'our dear member's' burdens.

Jane, planning future luncheons and dinners for Prudence and Fabian, thought for a moment that she was almost like Pandarus; but as everything was to be entirely decorous she decided that she was really more like Emma Woodhouse.

One scene is particularly reminiscent of *Emma*, and I think directly inspired. Mr Knightley, speaking to Emma of Mr Elton, says: 'from his general way of talking, in his unreserved moments, when there are only men present, I am convinced that he does not mean to throw himself away'. Thus Nicholas tells Jane: 'we had some conversation the other evening when he [Fabian Driver] was here to dinner; I understood then that he was not thinking of marrying again'.

'So that is what men talk about when they're alone together,' said Jane angrily. 'While Prue and I were struggling with the washing-up for six people you and Fabian were plotting that he should not marry again.'

But while Prudence is keeping up with Fabian – she has gone so far as to look at curtain materials and to choose a new wallpaper for Constance's room – Jessie Morrow from next door has made clandestine visits to him and has got further. Their engagement is announced. This has just been another of Prudence's love-affairs, but the breaking up has not been without some disappointment and humiliation, and some pain. Jane writes her a loving sympathetic letter, and Prudence is very kind and indulgent to herself over the next days. Geoffrey Manifold, who had noticed her distress, asked her to dinner on the Sunday – he will do as a stop-gap in her emotional life.

Jane, however, plans a new assault. Edward Lyall has spoken of Prudence with admiration. His house, 'the Towers', would be a better setting for Prudence than Fabian's little house on the green. Something was to come of this, for we learn in a later novel that Prudence had been engaged to a Member of Parliament (*GB*), but that the engagement had been broken off. In the same book we have a last glimpse of her having a mild flirtation with Wilmet's husband.

Mrs Glaze (who does some of Jane's cooking) thought that Jessie might have 'stooped to ways that Miss Bates wouldn't have dreamed of'. Something of the kind had occurred to Jane, who rather shyly asked Prudence if she were Fabian's mistress. Prudence's answer may mean anything: 'Surely either one is or one isn't and there's no need to ask coy questions about it.' As John Bayley well writes: 'Jane longs to know, but knows also that she never will know, and this is the root of her feel for the richness of life, Barbara Pym does not know herself. Her imagination does not bother with the anticlimax of what happens in bed.'*

*The Life and Work of Barbara Pym, p. 57.

It does not matter; the value that does matter to us is the simple goodness of Jane: 'I don't really know how people behave these days.' And we are glad that she does not.

One thing to which Prudence would not have stooped was to share a fish tea with Fabian after the cinema; Jessie responded to his vulgar side and encouraged it.

They were probably happy together, although Jessie no doubt mocked at Fabian's 'burdens' – if he could think up any. Years later (*FGL*) in the announcement of his death in the *Daily Telegraph* Jessie wrote: '*DRIVER. Fabian Charlesworth*, Devoted husband of Constance and Jessie' – an unconventional notice, but not ludicrous and contradictory like the frequent 'Beloved widow of John Doe'. But the devotion had probably been on the wives' side.

A Note on Marriage

In the 'canon' there are seven marriages: Henry and Agatha (*STG*), Rocky and Helena (*EW*), Nicholas and Jane (*JP*), Wilmet and Rodney, and Harry and Rowena (*GB*), Aylwin and Marjorie (*NFR*), and Mark and Sophia (*UA*). We may count in, if we please, Fabian and Constance (*JP*), though that union has been dissolved by death. Other characters marry marginally (as it were) – Digby and Deirdre, Everard and Mildred (but not in the books where they properly belong, and their marriages are not important).

Of all these marriages only one (Aylwin and Marjorie) is irretrievably broken; Rocky and Helena reunite after a short interval. There is no tyrannical husband (the Archdeacon does not quite get to that), and no nagging wife. Nor is any married couple seriously troubled by in-laws such as the interfering mother-in-law, the cruel stepmother, the hostile sisters-in-law, the feckless brother-in-law always in debt, or the drunken uncle. A woman's life will go through the normal stages of romance, humdrum marriage, and cosy widowhood. Men are, indeed, selfish about their 'burden' (if they have any), but Harry and Rodney will have any typewriting they need done in their offices, and several other husbands will not need any to be done. The Pym couples, by and large, are not examples of unhappy marriage.

Too much is written about Barbara's 'ambivalent' attitude to marriage; eager students appear to cross the Atlantic to 'research' into it. Whereas any English reader knowing something about life and literature could note on a half sheet of paper all that was necessary to explain this ugly neologism. Anyone with a little experience and observation must know perfectly well that some marriages are happy, some are not, and others are betwixt and between – that people like gossiping about them, and that gossip is rarely charitable. It is also probable that Barbara when young expected and wished one day to be married, and likely that in the end she was very well content with single blessedness.

Some things , however, seem to be forgotten by young students. The world changes, but many out-of-date ideas and prejudices survive their use and meaning. In the time of Jane Austen marriage was the only job for a gentlewoman (apart from the distressing alternatives of being a governess, a schoolmistress or a companion to an old lady); it was also her provision for the future. Jane Austen and her sister had to rely largely on their brothers' generosity.

Jane Austen's *Emma* was ahead of her time in asserting that spinsterdom (if unaccompanied by poverty) could be an honorable and desirable state. Many people have not yet got so far, and even Eleanor Hitchens (*JP*) with 'her flat in Westminster, so convenient for the Ministry, her weekend golf, concerts and theatres with women friends, in the best seats and with a good supper afterwards' might still be thought by her mother's friends to have 'missed marriage', at which she never aimed. And even a reunion of former students of a university (which must have sought to train the teachers and not the mothers of the race) is full of the old prejudice.

Nevertheless Eleanor thinks that Prudence ought to get married – it would settle her. It is time for her to stop having romantic love-affairs before she is too old for them. For her a good humdrum marriage might do very well, *mutatis mutandis*, like that of Jane and Nicholas, which has lasted long enough for their daughter to go up to Oxford, and seems certain to endure, despite little irritations between them from time to time. Prudence (had she pulled it off) might have done nearly as well with Fabian (both parties being proportionately inferior to Jane and Nicholas) and have ended in comfortable widowhood, as Jessie seems to have done.

We are told by a critic that 'men evade marriage when they can', but are often trapped into it by women; the latter take 'precedence' in it and 'husbands [exist] only in relation to them'.* A reference to context reveals that it is in the magazine of a women's college that the husbands' names naturally take second place – the readers will be interested to know whom their former fellow students have married. Similarly a magazine of a men's college will give the wives' names the second place.

The same commentator tells us: Driver's first wife, Jessie learns, had typed his MSS for him. 'Oh, then, he had to marry her . . . that kind of devotion is worse than blackmail – a man has no escape from that.' Fabian had no manuscripts, and there is no sign that Constance ever typed anything: the situation is carelessly lifted from *Excellent Women* where Mildred did some typing for Everard Bone.

In the same essay it is almost suggested that women do not get enough to eat. It is perhaps true that men have larger appetites than women. In hotels it was not uncommon to give men larger pieces of chicken, while women were compensated by being served more delicately with the white meat. I have heard a waiter call out to the kitchen the numbers of each sex. Pym men certainly have their appetites indulged, and Nicholas quite expects to be given two fried eggs at the Spinning Wheel, while his wife gets only one.

*The Life and Work of Barbara Pym, p. 90.

It is true that Arthur Grampian, Prudence Bates's boss, eats smoked salmon 'for dinner at his club' (in fact, it is for luncheon). Prudence, we learn, has to choose between shepherd's pie and stuffed marrow in a restaurant. But we also learn that Geoffrey Manifold, Grampian's assistant, has the same choice before him, in the same restaurant. Age and income, not gender, are here operative, and neither of them would be eligible for the club. Prudence is not being ill-treated and badly fed by a masculine world. The old adage 'always verify your references' must always be in the minds of those who read (or write) books about Barbara Pym – the mistakes and misunderstandings are as rife as if she were a writer of a distant age. Some of the worst have already been noted – and there are more to come.

[6]

The Anthropologists

Barbara noted that this novel, 'Less than Angels', was 'about the anthropologists',* but they are something like a static chorus; the chief interest in this book is that it is the one occasion (in the 'canon') when she wrote what was nearly a love-story. This would not have been essentially different had the principal male character been obliged to go overseas and to meet with danger by some other profession or interest.

It was through the chance recommendation of a friend that Barbara joined the International African Institute. She admitted that she had no degree in anthropology, though she had mastered its esoteric terminology,† of which she was frequently to make fun. She was a capable and conscientious editor of *Africa*, the Institute's journal, but 'had no real interest in Africa as such, being far more interested in the anthropologists and the linguists than by the subjects they were studying'.‡ It may be doubted if she knew as much as Deirdre, the first-year student, who is her secondary heroine. 'It is surely appropriate', wrote Barbara,§ 'that anthropologists, who spend their time studying life and behaviour in various societies, should be studied in their turn.' The nature and limitation of her study must later be examined.

*A Very Private Eye, p. 92.
†The Life and Work of Barbara Pym, p. 168.
‡A Very Private Eye, p. 183.
§Cover note to Less than Angels.

The love-story takes first place. Catherine Oliphant, who is the heroine, hardly seems to claim that position, though the book begins and ends with her. She was small and somewhat 'Bohemian' in appearance, without family, and self-employed. She earned a living by writing articles and sentimental stories for women's magazines; and though she drew her inspiration from everyday life, life itself was 'sometimes too strong and raw and must be made palatable by fancy, as tough meat may be made tender by mincing'. She made it very tender. 'Dear as remembered kisses after death,' says one character to another – a strikingly meaningless quotation from Tennyson's address to 'the days that are no more'. And yet Catherine is not ill-read and, though she writes trash herself, she knows how English should be written, and is justly critical of her lover's thesis.

Tom Mallow, her lover, was a young man who had broken away from his 'county' origins to 'study a tribe' and write a thesis on it. He had met Catherine on a channel crossing, stayed with her instead of looking for a room, and continued to do so whenever he was in London. As his fellow students sum it up: 'a woman who can cook *and* type – what more could a man want really?' And 'It would be a reciprocal relationship – the woman giving the food and shelter and doing some typing for him and the man giving the priceless gift of himself.' A typical programme for a Pym man.

Tom is now in England for some months. At the school of anthropology he meets a first-year student, Deirdre Swan, who falls headlong in love with him. Deirdre has many advantages: she is tall and pretty, ten years younger than Catherine, and able to take part in anthropological conversation or at least to listen to it with an appearance of interest. This, though attractive to a young male anthropologist, must mean very little to the reader, who cannot see her, and hears no amusing remark from her; 'I always think' is her usual preface, and her thoughts are never of any consequence. The author, aware of this, has carefully built up a background for her; and in our pleasure in Deirdre's home life we can almost forget Catherine, who has none.

Deirdre, a conventional young 'intellectual', would like to escape from suburbia, which she thinks 'stifling', into a life like Catherine's in London, though 'on the shabby side of Regent's Park'. While Catherine, going to tea at Deirdre's house, 'was delighted with the tranquillity of the Sunday afternoon scene, the tree-lined road, the neat colourful front gardens, some empty in the sunshine, others being vigorously tended by men in open-necked shirts or women in cotton dresses and sandals. Through it all came the pleasant sounds of children, dogs, birds, lawn-mowers and hedge-clippers.'

But even Deirdre, though 'not detached enough to appreciate any of the beauties of the scene', the wallflowers and tulips, the lilacs and laburnum, was glad of an evening to close her anthropological book, and to go downstairs. 'There was something reassuring about the scene; her mother and aunt sewing and knitting in the pleasant chintzy room cluttered with photographs and ornaments, the silver tea-tray and the gay tartan tin of shortbread on the little oak table. Deirdre felt comforted without realising that she had been in need of it.' Her mother and aunt have the cosiness of Belinda and Harriet Bede (*STG*); it was an ordered, affectionate, Christian household, very friendly with the vicar, Father Tulliver.

One evening Catherine, going into a Cypriot restaurant much frequented by Tom and herself, saw Tom and Deirdre holding hands. It is not sufficiently explained why she took this so seriously. She knew that Tom had been difficult, dissatisfied with his work, and that there she could give him little sympathy; she knew that Deirdre's obvious devotion was flattering and that he was flirtatious. If she had waited she must have won, had they been in competition. Possibly she feared his losing faith in her, and preferred to bring on a crisis. She took it unnecessarily for granted that he would need some place where he could be alone with Deirdre, but, unpossessive as she was, she might have left him to arrange that for himself.

There was no need to push him out of her flat into lodgings. It is not as if she were jealous, or had any ethical or social reasons for ending their liaison. We cannot be sure of her motives, though we may suggest some for her.

Tom was far from eager:

'I don't have to go, you know. I didn't mean to start off all this, and I don't think I did. It seems to be all your idea.'

'But it's a good idea, and you'll be able to finish your thesis much better away from me.'

She packed him off promptly.

Tom wanted freedom and an uncomplicated life. 'He had not left Catherine because he intended to embark on the same kind of relationship with Deirdre, whatever Catherine might have thought.' Deirdre with her background will obviously not become his mistress, and he as obviously will not want to be engaged or married to her. But she is young and possessive, and does not like Tom to keep in touch with Catherine. It will be seen that her infatuation with Tom was an adolescent impulse that will soon die away.

Life went on for Catherine: 'She thought of it as an old friend, or perhaps a tiresome elderly relative, pushing, clinging, but never leaving her alone, having the power to grant her moments of happiness, but being very stingy with them just now.'

Having made the breach, she resisted all temptation to heal it, though she could certainly have done so on more than one occasion; we are never shown her feeling that it had been entirely unnecessary. The temptation might have been acute had she known that Tom considered her such a strong, self-sufficient person that she could not be thought of as pathetic. Tom wept when he left her flat, but he did not know that she had. It would be even more annoying to know that Tom and Deirdre soothed their consciences about her by saying 'she has her writing'. She knew what her writing was worth.

Tom flew back to Africa, having finished his thesis. At the

airport he impartially embraced the two young women. He was glad to go. Catherine had said to him sardonically: 'How soothing it will be to get away from all this complexity of personal relations to the simplicity of a primitive tribe, whose only complications are in their kinship structure and rules of land tenure, which you can observe with the anthropologist's calm detachment.' For it is the anthropologist's first commandment: 'No expression of disgust, astonishment or amusement must show on the face of the investigator.'

Catherine likens the airport to a crematorium; and, though glad to go, Tom is somewhat fey. We are almost prepared for it when he is killed by accident, the police having been obliged to open fire during a riot. He died, like John Akenside (*STG*), as a spectator.

Catherine, in real grief, hastens to Deirdre's house to break the news. Deirdre is out, fortunately with a young fellow student who will do this for her and to whom she will soon transfer her affections. Her aunt and mother receive Catherine most kindly and make her stay. 'She was cosseted and cared for and almost knew what it was to be one of a family. In that short time she experienced all the cosiness and irritation which can come from living with thoroughly nice people with whom one has nothing in common.' It had done her great good, of which not the least part was to send her back thankfully to her 'odd solitary life'.

Deirdre, who had worn herself out with crying when Tom went away, seems drained of all feeling and clings to her fellow student, Digby Fox, who was at hand to comfort her. Catherine's sacrifice had evidently not been worth while. At one time, watching church workers bustling about, she had imagined there might be a place for her among them – 'but even she knew something of what it would involve and she did not feel she could face it yet, Like one of the saints ... but it seemed an irreverent comparison'. It was St Augustine who said 'not yet'. Few fictional characters know even as much as that, and perhaps not many of their creators. Catherine is the first of Barbara's characters whom we see in prayer (Mildred once went into church for 'consolation', but was soon interrupted); and, convincingly, she does not know how to pray. But Barbara will not leave her comfortless. If she is not ready for religion she can find some amusement in the wrecks of science, forming an odd friendship with Alaric Lydgate, Deirdre's neighbour and Gertrude's brother, who has brought back a quantity of masks from Africa.

We first met Deirdre in an anthropological library, with her fellow students Mark and Digby, friends of Tom – who was shortly expected to return from 'the field'. We meet other anthropologists, senior and junior, but only hear of the shabby 'hangers-on', former students of the department, and we do not see them.

> They lived in the meaner districts of London or in impossibly remote suburbs on grants which were always miserably inadequate, their creative powers stifled by poverty and family troubles. It would need the pen of a Dostoievsky to do justice to their dreadful lives.... Some of them had been fortunate enough to win the love of devoted women ... [who] had learned early in life what it is to bear love's burdens, listening patiently to their men's troubles and ever ready at their typewriters should a manuscript or even a short article get to the stage of being written down.

Anthropology becomes for its students a background to their thoughts and its 'esoteric terminology' provides a sort of humorous mythology.

In the decay of learning there must grow up many individual mythologies to take the place of the classical background that at one time was the common heritage of all educated people. Thus Barbara had used English poetry. Now she may have been the first writer to make this use of anthropological jargon. It escaped her once, inappropriately (*JP*), but in this book she could let it run riot.

One or two examples may suffice. Deirdre's brother Malcolm frequented the local club, where the young men of the neighbourhood gathered for mysterious manly purposes. Deirdre was reminded of the African men's associations which she had read about in the course of her studies. But the object of these seemed to be to intimidate the women, whereas here women were allowed to belong to some sections of the club and might almost be considered as one of its amenities. Perhaps they intimidated the men. Certainly they often led them captive in marriage and Malcolm had recently become engaged to a girl he had met when playing tennis.

Mark Penfold gave up anthropology, and was going to work in the office of his future father-in-law in Leadenhall Street.

'*Leadenhall Street!*' hissed Miss Clovis. 'The very sound of it is dreadful. And yet one is reminded even there of the African custom of the suitor giving service to the father of the girl he wishes to marry, but *Leadenhall* Street' – she seemed unable to leave the name alone – 'that's rather different from raising the mounds for the yams.'

Barbara may not have known much about anthropology, but she knew what anthropology was about: it was about things like matrilineal kin-groups, or the functions of the father's brother, kinship structure and rules of land tenure. Barbara could not have been an anthropologist, for these subjects seemed to her unimportant and boring. Even attempts to save an almost extinct language or a dying culture from disappearance could not have mattered to her, given the sort of language or culture at issue. It was the sort of language and culture that only anthropologists would know about.

Tom is misunderstood by some readers. He 'used to move in the world of débutante dances before he saw the light and detribalized himself', and stood one night outside a terrace of large houses in Belgravia, where an aunt of his was giving a ball that he did not

[65]

care to attend. But he felt depressed 'about seeing rows of filing-cabinets in what had been somebody's drawing-room, trestle tables standing on parquet floors; wire trays and even a thick white cup and saucer glimmering faintly in the moonlight. If we lamented the decay of the great civilizations of the past, he thought, should we not also regret the dreary levelling down of our own?'

The 'great civilizations' have never been the care of anthropology. And it is as a gentleman not as an anthropologist that Tom regrets the decay of our own. He is not completely 'detribalized'. The thick white cup is more than he can tolerate. Once he had probably drunk exquisite China tea from eggshell china in such a drawing-room. 'Oh, death in life, the days that are no more!'

A confusion between the nature of anthropological observation and what we may call 'detective investigation' is frequent among critics of Barbara Pym, and it must be admitted that sometimes she inadvertently gave cause for it. 'Investigation' was a favourite hobby of hers, from early years, long before she had thought of Africa. Her methods were sometimes in some ways analogous with those of anthropologists, but on the whole they were directed at different subjects, individuals and the 'complexity of personal relations' – very different from the more or less rigid conventions of a primitive tribe. It is interesting that her 'private investigators' (if we may so call them, and they include herself) are generally far more observant than the scientists. Mildred (*EW*), Rhoda Wellcome and Mrs Swan, and Catherine Oliphant (*LA*) are the keenest observers in the novels. Such observation would not be very useful to science, and it is in very old-fashioned books such as *Five Years with the Congo Cannibals* that use is made of it. Modern works are less readable in consequence.

'The untrained observer from another culture often misses the significance of what he observes.'* This is often obvious in the

---

*The Life and Work of Barbara Pym, p. 104.

work of transatlantic critics of Barbara Pym, but she never missed the significance of what she observed.

When such a lack of training is combined with a total lack of humour (for it must not be forgotten that Barbara was not always serious) the result can be as ridiculous as the critical pages devoted to Jean-Pierre Le Rossignol and his visit to Deirdre's family.

Jean-Pierre is in London for the sake of the Institute, and is a fellow pupil of Deirdre and others. He is not 'studying' the English, of whom he has a perfect comprehension, and if he deliberately shows off his satisfaction at being a Frenchman, who can blame him? Someone wonders why English women do not marry – Jean-Pierre glances round the room and says, 'Need you ask?' Like most foreign visitors (and many English people) he finds the English Sunday intolerable. But he has thought out a plan for getting through it by visiting a number of churches.

'Last week I was at a Methodist Chapel – exquisite.... The week before at the Friends' House. Next Sunday I have been recommended to try Mattins and Sermon at a fashionable church in Mayfair.' On Whit Sunday he turns up at Father Tulliver's church, to which Deirdre had half-invited him, for he had not yet studied 'the Sunday morning in the English suburb'.

He is presumably an unbeliever, though he says he is a Thomist, but his behaviour is entirely respectful. If he is not dressed much like everyone else, but rather better, he is not there as an anthropologist, carefully avoiding attention. Deirdre's family are pleased to see him; he 'put his questions about English suburban life so charmingly that nobody could possibly have taken offence'.

He is told that Deirdre's mother and aunt are washing up after luncheon.

'I see; the older female relatives work in the kitchen when there are no servants. The mother and the father's sister?'

'No, Aunt Rhoda is my mother's sister.'

'Ah, yes, I understand. Women more closely linked would work better together – they would not fight.'

They do indeed have their little skirmishes, and this is part of Barbara's irony; but Jean-Pierre may not be so far wrong. He goes off to 'a meeting in Bayswater, a message from the Other Side'. He affects to think that all the English sleep after eating their joint at Sunday luncheon – but this is his little joke. And if he goes to Bournemouth to observe the English on holiday, he knows quite well that there are other resorts.

He is playing an amusing little anthropological game, and is only carrying it further than any of the other characters.

Another amusing anthropological diversion – a short story in itself, and completely detachable from the main stories in the book – is provided by Felix Mainwaring, a distinguished senior anthropologist. He invites four candidates for special grants to spend a weekend in his country house, and there applies something like the legendary tests offered to candidates for the Foreign Service, or for fellowships at All Souls. Mark and Digby and two young women are brought there to be tried, but in the end it has all been in vain, for a rival scholar has got round the benefactress and obtained the funds.

The Clergy House

When she started on *A Glass of Blessings* Barbara wrote to me that her new novel was to be about a clergy house; and perhaps that theme at first dominated her imagination. She had referred to *Less than Angels* as a book about the anthropologists, but we have seen that they do not really provide the principal theme. But Jane Austen said she was writing about 'ordination', and the novel was *Mansfield Park*.

There is again a first-person narrator, but a very different character from Mildred (*EW*).

Wilmet Forsyth, the heroine and narrator, is described on the fly-leaf as a 'rather selfish and frivolous young woman', and she would not quarrel with this description. But she is pleasant and kindly, entirely unpretentious, and if she thinks chiefly of herself there is no one and nothing – apart from 'good causes' – that particularly demands her thought. Rodney, her rather dull husband, seems to have no interests outside his work; Sybil, her mother-in-law, takes the household management on her own shoulders, as well as having archaeological interests and taking part in various 'good works' – but the latter, she tells her daughter-in-law, are 'something for one's old or middle age, not really for youth'. Wilmet has far too little to do, and in consequence she is rather bored, as more 'excellent women' have no time to be. She is perhaps the only 'frustrated woman' in the Pym world, and it is worth remarking that it is a married woman who is in this position;

spinsters are never so unoccupied.

Barbara one day was surprised to hear a telephone ring in the church of St Mary Aldermary. It had no particular significance for her, but she thought it would make a good beginning for a novel – and so it does.

Wilmet, who lives in an unbelieving world, is an Anglo-Catholic: she may have been brought up so, for her Christian name comes from a novel by Charlotte Yonge. At the beginning of the book she is at a late mass at St Luke's church on its patronal festival (18 October) which is also her thirty-third birthday. She is struck by the ringing of the telephone, and we may (tidily but inexactly) say that in a way it summons her to Sacred and Profane Love.

At the church door she gets into conversation for the first time with the vicar, Father Thames, who tries to interest her in church activities. Then she is addressed by Piers Longridge, brother of her great friend Rowena, once a fellow officer with her in the Wrens. Piers teaches French and Portuguese at an evening institute, and has a job as a proof-reader for French and Portuguese books – not very well-paid or much-esteemed posts. He was thought not to have fulfilled his youthful brilliance and to have 'something unsatisfactory' about him.

Barbara deals skilfully with Piers's homosexuality. It is not a mystery or a problem, but it is necessary for the story that Wilmet should not realize it until the right moment, and then that this knowledge should shed light over all the past. Nevertheless, though the reader is at once convinced at the revelation, of which he was perhaps in no need, he does not think Wilmet a fool for neglecting obvious clues, for they were not so obvious as that. It is what (ignorantly perhaps) I call the 'crime-club technique'. This was triumphantly employed by Jane Austen. Emma must not know until the right moment that there is an understanding between Frank Churchill and Jane Fairfax, though John Knightley has his suspicions, and on rereading we find many hints. Emma collaborates in her own deception, and so (in a smaller way) does Wilmet, who imagines Piers sharing a flat with a colleague.

Rowena is inclined to commend Piers to her: 'I'm sure it would be so good for him to have a nice female friend.' If she knows any more about her brother she does not reveal it until the end of the book. But she does wonder if his friends are 'of the right kind'.

Barbara knew very well, both by experience and observation, how valuable and happy a friendship can be between a woman and a homosexual man – but it is necessary that Eros should not intervene and spoil it all; and if he does not, what becomes of the story? Twice she has given her heroine an unreturned feeling for a man – but the stories are very different. Leonora (*SDD*) must be reserved for later (and severer) treatment.

Wilmet, though more sympathetic, is in a way more culpable. She does not think she wants to be more than a good friend, and (at need) a ministering angel to Piers – and also believes that she is a respectable married woman. She ought, then, not to feel aggrieved when she finds the boy Keith in possession. She had even thought Piers might be living with another woman – did she hope to dislodge her? However, it appears that all passion is soon spent, and a happy friendship seems to follow in a later novel.

Piers enjoyed the innocent flirtation between them and the conversation of someone more amusing and sophisticated than anyone he normally met. He shared some interests with her – he was an occasional church-goer, and knew enough about English poetry to make an apt quotation. His ordinary world was very banal and dreary. He never deceived Wilmet in any way, not having Frank Churchill's motive for deception.

Wilmet had certainly helped to brighten Piers's life, which involved the dreariest forms of teaching and literary activity; but the improvement in his spirits, which she believed due to herself, was in fact due (it is suggested) to a change in his private life, and the replacement of an unsatisfactory partner by the undemanding Keith. Like Wilmet, we are bored by the common, flat voice and the lack of ideas – and he is so vividly described that we can almost share her pleasure in looking at him, but it is remarkable that he and Piers should have remained so long together as later they seem to have done.

It would be unfair to Wilmet to suppose that she wished to become Piers's mistress – though she almost laid herself open to such an invitation. Her disappointment was more in herself than for him – evidently she was less charming, less necessary to his life than she thought. As she says to her friend Mary, who has noticed her loss of self-confidence: 'Sometimes you discover that you aren't as nice as you thought you were – that you're in fact rather a horrid person, and that's humiliating somehow.'

At first she was surprised at Keith's welcome of her; he had no reason at all to fear her as a rival, and indeed was pleased to visit her and discuss household hints and the choice of stuff for curtains with her. He himself was sometimes employed as a model, and in the evenings worked in a coffee bar, but spent a great deal of time and trouble keeping Piers's rather miserable lodgings in a state of spotless cleanliness.

Wilmet's increased interest in church activities was well timed, though some weeks before the beginning of the Church's year. Father Thames lives in the clergy house with the good, pious, common little Father Bode. But two new assistants are coming. The cook-housekeeper, Mrs Greenhill, is leaving on account of fibrositis and is to be replaced by Wilfrid Bason, an unsuccessful employee of Rodney's ministry. Wilmet has heard that he is a fine cook, and is responsible for his appointment. Mrs Greenhill had no ideas beyond cod and cabbage, but Bason is a gourmet, and original even eccentric in his cuisine – one cannot help wondering if his octopus fried in batter can really be a success – could an octopus be sufficiently beaten? His other eccentricity is a strange form of kleptomania. He takes small valuable objects without any attempt at concealment, or any intention of not giving them back.

The other newcomer is a second curate, Father Marius Lovejoy Ransome. He is a handsome young man who has previously served in the East End and in the worst part of North Kensington, but he appears to be socially well suited to this comparatively comfortable parish. Like Father Thames he is a man of taste, but he is no intellectual (we learn later that he took a third in theology), and is an uninspired preacher.

Father Thames is unwilling to make room for him at the clergy house, although he has his meals there with the other priests – except for breakfast which he prepares for himself at his lodgings. He lodges very near, in two spare rooms in the neighbouring flat of old Mrs Beamish. It is unexplained why she, who is very well off, is prepared to accept a lodger. It is unlikely that she was persuaded into this (or anything else) by her daughter Mary, a super-excellent woman, and a 'do-gooder' of the most irritating kind. Mary is much oppressed and hard worked by her grumbling old mother, but she is a kind friend to Wilmet and unconsciously does her the further kindness of making elegance and harmless frivolity look very attractive when compared with dowdy unselfishness. She is so full of good works that she feels 'quite dashing' if she has a free afternoon; but though her charity begins at church it does not end there. Wilmet slightly resents her for being so much 'immersed' in good works that she herself feels particularly useless by comparison.

Mary persuades Wilmet to be a blood donor: 'It's great fun.' This is much to say, though it is a harmless and for Wilmet a new experience. She is then asked to help Mary to buy 'a sort of wool dress suitable for parish evening occasions' – a depressing estimate of Mary's social life. Wilmet takes a good deal of trouble, and wonders why: 'For when one came to think of it what did it matter what she wore? She might just as well buy a dress as much like her old blue as possible, for all the difference it would make in her life.' Wilmet chose a becoming black dress and some artificial pink pearls to 'dress up the neckline'. It is not improbable that this free afternoon has made all the difference in Mary's life. It is clear that she is becoming interested in Marius Ransome.

The church environment (some of which overlaps with the Settlement, run by Sybil, who is agnostic) falls roughly into two classes. The gentry consist of Father Thames and Father Ransome, of Sir Denbigh Grote (a retired ambassador), of Miss Prideaux

[73]

(who has in her time been a governess in royal and imperial households), and of several ladies who are hardly mentioned. The other class consists of the admirable Father Bode, of Bill Coleman who is the master of ceremonies, and a number of altar-servers – of the English lower middle class and the salt of the earth. The elaborate and beautiful services of the church – which they carry out to perfection – might be a compensation for the greyness of their lives as garage hands or elementary schoolteachers – but do not seem to move them to the appreciation of other beauty.

Wilfrid Bason seems to be in a class by himself. He invites Rodney and Wilmet to tea on Boxing Day. While they are enjoying a delicious meal with him at the clergy house, Father Ransome telephones to announce old Mrs Beamish's death. This creates a crisis; Father Ransome cannot stay in his lodgings while Mary is 'unchaperoned'. He is taken in by Father Edwin Sainsbury, the vicar of a nearby parish – but Father Sainsbury is much disturbed by the question of inter-communion with the Church of South India, and in fact 'goes over' to Rome in consequence. Mary, meanwhile, has gone to the convent of St Hildelith to 'try her vocation'.

In May, in a happy dream of looking after Piers, Wilmet took a train to visit the convent to see Mary. It is odd that with her High Church upbringing Wilmet is scared of nuns and convents. She finds Mary unsettled and beginning to feel that she will leave the convent. She is also worried about Marius Ransome, who has written her letters full of doubts and questionings, disturbed by Edwin Sainsbury's leanings towards Rome; he seems to be in need of her, though it is extraordinary to think that Mary can help here. Was it possible, Wilmet thought, that Marius and Mary might marry? She dismissed the idea at once: 'Obviously if he went over to Rome he would want to go on being a priest and therefore couldn't marry anybody. And even if he stayed where he was and decided to marry, he would choose somebody younger and more attractive than Mary.'

Father Bode suggested that Mary might get a job as housekeeper

[74]

in a house for retreats – a life more independent but not much more worldly than that of the convent. Wilmet invites her to stay while she is making the change.

On the day of her meeting with Keith and her disillusionment with Piers, Wilmet returns home to find Mary already arrived for her visit. Mary finds her a little depressed, but her company, which prevents her from talking about Piers, is probably the best thing for her. She is taking it a little too hard, and may begin to feel that she has overrated her own charm and underrated that of Mary.

Apart from Catherine (*LA*) Wilmet is the only one of Barbara's heroines whom we see praying, though we do not go more deeply into her spiritual life than to follow her intercessory prayers, or once to hear of her saying 'one of those indefinite prayers which come to us if we are at all used to praying and which can impose themselves above other thoughts, so often totally unconnected with spiritual matters'. This is significant, for now that we know Wilmet is 'used to praying' we are entitled to think the same of other church-going (and often more excellent) people in the 'canon' and to refute the critics who choose to think otherwise. Moreover we see prayer as part of a Christian's daily life – as few novelists show it. It is not only a refuge in time of crisis (as it was for Catherine), and not the prerogative of saints or great sinners, but a constant background to 'the trivial round, the common task', or even to Wilmet's lack of these.

Mary and Wilmet help to decorate St Luke's, covering the floor with leaves and flowers for the great candle-light Corpus Christi procession. Julian Malory has been invited to preach, and probably does so better than any of the parish clergy would. No doubt some of our old friends from St Mary's (*EW*) come to hear him, though we only notice Sister Blatt. Father Thames makes a semi-farewell address. He is going on his holiday to Italy and will probably resign on his return.

In that case the clergy house, as we have known it, will revert to banality. Marius has gone to the Retreat House and proposed to Mary, who accepts him, in spite of her feeling that priests should not marry – a feeling that might have been even stronger had she heard Father Thames's reception of this news: 'It's too bad, too bad!' Or had she had heard Bason say, 'Celibacy of the Clergy has always been our motto.'

We feel, perhaps, that the novel ends too quickly and too thoroughly. Mary's story cannot be as strong an interest as Wilmet's – a much more conventional theme, a young man marrying his landlady's daughter, and the success of a dowdy and earnest young woman in attracting a handsome man – but it is meant to set off Wilmet's disappointment, and teaches her a lesson, or underlines that which she has received from Piers. It is a happy thing that her mother-in-law, Sybil, has decided to marry her old friend Professor Arnold Root. Wilmet and Rodney will now have to take a flat or house of their own, and that will give her an occupation which she will not dislike – Keith will want to be even too helpful over the furnishing. Moreover Rodney and Wilmet, now on their own, find their marriage coming to life again – an edifying conclusion although perhaps Wilmet loses in interest by it, while Rodney gains no more.

Meanwhile Father Thames will be settling in his new villa La Cenerentola near Siena – where, though he is only a tenant, he has installed a new bath of Carrara marble. In another Cenerentola, a coffee bar near Marble Arch, Keith works the machine in the evening and serves 'Danish pastries' in an 'Italian décor'. Father Bode will now be vicar of St Luke's and out of devotion to him Mrs Greenhill will return to make his strong tea and cook his cod and cabbage – the clergy house will no longer require Wilfrid Bason and his beautiful cooking.

Bason rather comes down in the world. He is going to an antique shop in Devonshire that 'does teas' in the season. Wilmet and Rodney on a motor tour visit the shop and find Bason bearded and wearing a blue smock frock, but he has to serve lobster salad for tea (surely very lower class) and tinned fruit – very different from the scampi of the clergy house dinner.

Marius and Mary are quietly married, as befits two people who had almost taken vows of celibacy. We are not present, but the entertainment which brings all our friends together for a farewell chapter is the induction of Father Ransome into his new parish church somewhere in the suburbs – an ending of the sort favoured by Barbara.

Life, says Mary, is 'a glass of blessings', and Wilmet does not see why her own should not become the same. She still feels a little guilty about the excessive interest she formerly took in Piers, and Rodney confesses to a similar interest in Prudence (imported from *PJ*). This is very good for Wilmet who had taken for granted that he would never look at another woman, and was perhaps surprised at another woman looking at him. She has been slightly improved, but was not in need of drastic improvement – one fears she will not be interesting any more. This novel, unlike most of the 'canon', does not seem to end with Gide's favourite conclusion: *pourrait être continué*.

Characters from earlier novels appear off the scene. Sometimes one is glad to meet old friends, sometimes it is a mistake. As Philip Larkin wrote: 'the conversation between Wilmet and Rowena . . . about Rocky Napier is only meaningful if we have met him in *Excellent Women*'.* Rowena, at the hairdresser's, picks up 'Sunday Evening', a story by Catherine Oliphant in a glossy magazine. We know that it was a transcription from life and that poor Catherine (*LA*) was describing Tom and Deirdre in a Cypriot restaurant, and herself looking on. The comments of Rowena and Wilmet are amusingly ironical only if we know the former book.

Note

There is one passage which may puzzle readers.

'Wouldn't *believe* the trouble we had over them,' Mr Bason was saying. 'It's really simpler when you haven't got any,' said Mr

*Foreword to *An Unsuitable Attachment*.

Coleman in his low voice with its slightly north country accent. 'There were only four Sundays in Advent last year, I remember, so it can be a bit of a problem when to use them.'

They are the rose-coloured vestments worn at Mid-Advent and Mid-Lent, as a change from the violet of the season, to encourage the Faithful. There is really no problem, and Coleman was liturgiologist* enough to know this, as the fixed days are *Gaudete* Sunday, third in Advent, and *Laetare* Sunday, fourth in Lent. The days are named from their introits in the mass. There are seldom more than four Sundays in Advent, so it more often than not has no middle – but this passage seems to date 'last year' as 1956 or 1957. There is a nostalgic pleasure to be derived from the problems of Bason and Coleman; few people, one fears, are likely to be faced with them today, now the Church is 'rob'd and tore'.

It was in St Mary Aldermary that Barbara heard the telephone, but it seems that St Luke's owes most to All Saints', Notting Hill.

---

*He knows that the Paschal Candle ought to be removed after the Gospel on Ascension Day.

[8]

Investigation

Two of the heroines in the 'canon', Mildred (*EW*) and Wilmet (*GB*), are narrators, story-tellers, and therefore may be regarded as novelists of a kind; Jane Cleveland is a published author (although she has only written a book of essays), and Catherine Oliphant (*LA*) writes sentimental stories and appears to live by them. But Dulcie Mainwaring, in *No Fond Return of Love*, belongs to an even humbler stratum of the literary world: 'I just do odd jobs and make indexes.' Of course we have all been told that a book is made or marred by its index – but still. . . . It is not the only way in which Dulcie fails to live up to the standard of the other heroines and, pleasant as the book is, one is obliged to feel (with Mr Charles Burkhart*) a 'falling-off' from the previous novels.

No Fond Return of Love, this is what Barbara's heroines may expect to get out of life. If not rather boringly married (Jane and Wilmet) they are shown as definitely without successful love. Belinda has her dream of the past; Mildred has not yet been in love and we do not know that she ever will be, though she will certainly marry; Patience has her 'love-affairs' as a rather unproductive hobby; Catherine is at the end of an affair, and Deirdre is in the grip of an adolescent infatuation; Wilmet fixes her affections where they are unwanted. Dulcie Mainwaring has out-distanced

---

*Charles Burkhart, *The Pleasure of Miss Pym*, University of Texas Press, Austin, 1987, p. 44.

them all, for she begins with a broken heart.

Maurice, a beautiful young man, had broken their engagement, saying that he was not 'worthy' of her. Probably he was not. Dulcie's heartbreak was not the sort one dies of.

Theirs would have been one of those rather dreadful marriages, with the wife a little older and a little taller and a great deal more intelligent than the husband. Yet although she was laughing, there was a small ache in her heart as she remembered him. Perhaps it is sadder to have loved someone 'unworthy', and the end of it is such a very little thing, like a child's coffin, she thought confusedly.

Dulcie has an inferior name, like Deirdre (at least I conjecture that Barbara may have thought so), and they were both suburban dwellers. Dulcie, however, unlike Deirdre, likes this. She has a house and a pleasant garden to herself and no family nearer than her sister's in Devonshire. She is in her early thirties and has taken a degree in English. Unlike many of Barbara's heroines she is not a regular church-goer. This lack in her, in some indefinable way, detracts from her interest and coherence – we take her less seriously as a moral agent, and perhaps her author has less feeling for her. In this book the year passes, uncharted by the calendar of the Church's year. At Christmas one generally goes to stay with relations, at Easter one takes another break, but they are merely seasonal. Even Wilmet, with her parochial activities, becomes in comparison a more excellent woman. We miss a church as a focal point, and though we meet a priest he is almost off duty. At the end of the book we find that Dulcie may be tempted to marry a divorced man, and we do not feel quite confident that she will refuse – although he is not attractive enough to provide much excuse.

Dulcie, having no religious background, gives way to a sentimental compassion for the unfortunate, which Mildred would have turned into the motive for 'good works'. We are given one example of her wasting her pity on an impostor:

> She had seen a new and particularly upsetting beggar selling matches; both legs were in irons and he was sitting on a little stool, hugging himself as if in pain. She had given him sixpence and walked quickly on, telling herself firmly that there was no need for this sort of thing now, with the Welfare State.

Later she was to see him 'walking briskly in the evening sunshine, wearing a good suit'.

When she was beginning to recover from the loss of Maurice Dulcie used an original *remedium amoris*. She went to a conference for those who 'correct proofs, make bibliographies and indexes and do all the rather humdrum tasks for people more brilliant'. It is perhaps better for a broken heart than Barbara's own nostrum, Yeastvite,* or than the algebra book that Philip Morville in *The Heir of Redclyffe* advised Laura to work through.

Unfortunately the other members of the conference are, on the whole, as dull as the subjects of the lectures – 'Some Problems of Indexing' or the like. The men in this book are nearly all lacking in interest, and if Maurice, and Aylwin who succeeds him in Dulcie's affections, are very good-looking, this is no use to the reader, who cannot see them. The only woman who makes much impression on Dulcie is no better; Viola Dace is a pretentious, rather common young person of intellectual aspirations who likes to fancy that there is something 'between' herself and Aylwin Forbes, for whom she has done some secretarial work. However, Dulcie returns home after the conference with at least two people in whom her interest had been aroused – Aylwin, because of Viola's confidences and because he had fainted while lecturing on 'Some Problems of an Editor' – as the Professor of Poetry had done years ago at Oxford, when Barbara and I went to hear him lecture on Hopkins.

*A Very Private Eye, p. 25.

[81]

Dulcie's ruling passion is curiosity. 'I love finding out about people,' she said. 'I suppose it's a sort of compensation for the dreariness of everyday life.' And: 'Perhaps other people's lives are a kind of refuge . . . one can enjoy the cosiness of them.' In addition to indexing, Dulcie occasionally did research for a client in the British Museum or the Public Record Office. Now Aylwin became the object of a private research, always her favourite hobby.

She looked him up in the telephone directory. She might see him one day, though he did not live at all near. 'Perhaps . . . it would have to be contrived; women were often able to arrange things that men would have thought impossible.' Then, washing her hands in the cloakroom of a 'learned institution', she ran into a woman, previously met at the conference, who told her that Aylwin Forbes was her vicar's brother – a further clue.

For this was really the kind of research Dulcie enjoyed most of all, investigation – some might have said prying – into the lives of other people, the kind of work that involved pouring over reference books, and street and telephone directories. It was most satisfactory if the objects of her research were not too well known either to herself or to the world in general, for it was rather dull just to be able to look up somebody in *Who's Who*, which gave so many relevant details. *Crockford* was better because it left more to the imagination, not stooping to such personal trivia as marriages, children or recreations.

Dulcie looked up Neville Forbes in *Crockford*; his parish was in an accessible part of North London, 'almost within walking distance, if one were wearing comfortable shoes', of where her Uncle Bertram and her Aunt Hermione lived. 'Gross inc. 626*l*. and Ho' – she read. And house? Probably Aylwin and Neville Forbes had private means; there must be money in the family, for Aylwin can earn little from editing a learned journal and yet (we learn later) has funds to help his mother if she needs it.

Mr Burkhart puts down 'the omission' of money in Barbara's novels to 'a ladylike propriety'; I am afraid he means 'middle-class gentility', for Jane Austen, who was a little higher in the social scale, made no bones about it. But I do not think Barbara had as much reason to speak of money, as the 'dowry' does not enter into her plots.

It is odd that Dulcie should sigh for the coming of a time 'when one may be permitted to do research into the lives of ordinary people', and that no commentator on the 'canon' has remembered that the time had already come. As early as 1937 'Mass Observation' was in full swing, but, although I was aware of it, I do not recollect speaking of it with Barbara. Before her there were observers dedicated to an anthopological survey of their own society. 'We do not intend to intrude on the private life of the individual,' they declared.* 'Collective habits and social behaviour are our field of enquiry.' But, like Barbara, the founders of Mass Observation were marked by 'a passionate concern for "trifles" unconsidered by others, for the sights and smells of ordinary life going on irrespective of politicians and generals'.† Though the approach to field-work should be as objective as possible, Mass Observation 'assumed that its untrained Observers would be *subjective* cameras, each with his or her own distortion. They tell us not what society is like but what it looks like to them.'‡ Their intention was to show how people lived and thought, with the hope of bringing greater rationality into life, but perhaps the most important things they observed were oddities of individual behaviour, on which no generalizations could be based.

We may compare their intentions with those given to her anthropologists by Barbara (*LA*).

They went out to remote places and studied the customs and languages of the peoples living there. . . . And it was a very good

---

Speak for Yourself: A Mass Observation Anthology 1937–49, Angus Calder and Dorothy Sheridan (eds), Jonathan Cape, London, 1984, p. 64.
†Ibid p. 1.
‡Ibid., pp. 5–6.

thing that these languages and customs should be known, firstly because they were interesting in themselves and in danger of being forgotten, and secondly because it was helpful to missionaries and government officials to know as much as possible about the people they sought to evangelize or govern.

Barbara herself, however, in so far as she was an Observer (and she kept notebooks like an anthropologist) did 'intrude on the private life of the individual' in her kind of research. As an investigator she seldom spoke of 'collective habits or social behaviour', and certainly had no intention of being useful to anyone. Her language may sometimes borrow anthropological jargon, but in the 'canon' the tea-party of the Learned Society (*EW*) is unique in comparing two cultures. One of the members tells us: 'The so-called primitive peoples have an elaborate order and precedence in eating but I'm afraid that when we get started it is every man for himself.'

In *No Fond Return of Love*, Dulcie as an investigator is more like a literary scholar and a detective – and we may certainly say that she 'pries'.

No doubt Barbara had often cast her eyes over the reference books in the Bodleian and elsewhere. It is quite remarkable how much one can find out about people that way, even things they would rather conceal. Dulcie learned from *Who's Who* that Aylwin's wife had been Marjorie Williton, and he affectedly gave his recreations as 'conversation and wine'.

The telephone directory gave her the address of 'Williton, Mrs Grace' – probably Aylwin's mother-in-law. At all event she lived so near that it was worth trying. Dulcie went, and found a jumble sale in progress, in aid of the Organ Fund. And there was Marjorie Forbes in a 'mauve twin-set' – 'terribly difficult to wear': a young woman whose appearance made Dulcie think Aylwin had 'married beneath him'.

The organ was in Father Tulliver's church, for the Willitons lived in the same parish as the Swans. Dulcie met an old friend of ours, Rhoda Wellcome (from *LA*), who told her that Deirdre was married to Digby Fox and was expecting a baby – information of greater interest to readers of the previous book rather than to readers of this one. She also told her that Marjorie was living at home, having run away from Aylwin, whom she described as 'quite a libertine'. The silly girl had merely caught him comforting Viola Dace, who was in tears. Viola had also built up a romance on this foundation.

Dulcie also visited St Ivel's, Neville Forbes's church. Viola, who, having been turned out of her flat for untidiness, had come to lodge with Dulcie, could not understand why she was so inquisitive.

'No, but it's like a game,' said Dulcie. It seemed – though she did not say this to Viola – so much safer and more comfortable to live in the lives of other people – to observe their joys and sorrows in detachment as if one were writing a film or play.

'One goes on with one's research, avidly and without shame. Then suddenly a curious feeling of delicacy comes over one. One sees one's subjects – or perhaps victims is the better word – as being somehow degraded by our probings.'

Dulcie went, taking Viola with her, to solemn evensong and benediction at Neville's church. His housekeeper revealed that Father Forbes was away – he had probably gone (in flight from a woman who was pursuing him) to the West Country, where his mother kept a hotel at Taviscombe. Dulcie and Viola decided to spend Easter at Eagle House, Taviscombe (said to be based on Minehead).

Here, then, the research is always literary. Young anthropologists will not have earned any mention in reference books; one takes no interest in their families, and one cannot track them down in the distant field. If it was fitting to study them in terms of anthropology, it is fitting to study Aylwin Forbes in terms of his own intellectual activity, literary research. He is not a very rewarding subject, but then his subject is not very rewarding. He is devoting his labours to Edmund Lydden (a fictitious writer): 'one of that little band of neo-metaphysical poets of the late seventeenth and eighteenth centuries who have been curiously neglected by posterity'. But now it was hard to find a poet 'so obscure that not even the Americans had "done" him'. One can understand the neglect of 'posterity'.

At Easter Aylwin was believed to be in Italy; indeed he had sent a card to Dulcie's niece Laurel, to whom he had taken a fancy. It therefore seemed safe to go to Taviscombe, but Dulcie's curious feeling of delicacy obliged them first to spend a night at another hotel. They stayed at the Anchorage, although it advertised a 'Bright Christian Atmosphere', which they rightly thought uninviting. Their worst expectations were fulfilled. The horrible dinner was served at a quarter to seven. 'The silence of the room was broken only by the sound of water being poured into glasses – perhaps the most dismal sound heard on an English holiday.' There was bright red tomato soup accompanied by very small squares of white bread; this was followed (although it was Good Friday) by thin slices of meat and little dishes with just enough vegetables for two. Finally there were stewed plums and custard and thimble-sized cups of coffee.

For us the most important incident is the arrival of Barbara herself, who came to an unoccupied table; but 'as she was a woman of about forty, ordinary-looking and unaccompanied, nobody took much notice of her. As it happened, she was novelist; indeed some of the occupants of the tables had read and enjoyed her books, but it would never have occurred to them to connect her name, even if they had ascertained it from the hotel register, with that of the author they admired.' She could observe them without embarrassment.

The 'investigation' continues: the two friends stay at Eagle House, meet Aylwin's mother, the rather crafty Horatia Forbes, and his brother Neville. They see mother and son decorating the father's grave for Easter and learn that the latter had 'married into

[86]

the hotel', Horatia's heritage. Later, visiting the 'Castle', a hideous building of the last century, they learn from other visitors (who are our old friends Wilmet and Keith from *GB*) that the former owner, Miss Forbes, had disinherited her nephew (the father of Aylwin and Neville) for marrying 'the daughter of someone who kept a hotel in the town – quite a common sort of person'.

Then comes a development that is, I think, unique in the 'canon': Life outraces Research. Aylwin's wife Marjorie appears with her mother at Eagle House, almost immediately followed by Aylwin himself. It might have been predicted that Dulcie would find herself caught in the hotel lounge and have to hide behind a screen while Aylwin and the women had a final row. Later by the cold, grey sea she and Aylwin encountered each other. He confessed to being in love with her young niece Laurel, for which she severely scolded him.

Viola, as second heroine or confidante, does little to create an interest in her role. She easily gives up the pursuit of Aylwin and of all intellectual matters when she meets Bill Sedge (Wili Soj?) the brother of the cook in the household of Dulcie's aunt – an Austrian refugee and a knitwear salesman.

We are tempted to think that Dulcie might have had more interesting things to tell us if she had turned her observation more often to the house next door. This belonged to Mrs Beltane, 'an elegant, stiffly-moving woman of about sixty, who imagined herself to have seen better days'. She had let the top floor of her house to a Brazilian diplomat, Senhor MacBride Pereira. Mrs Beltane has a horrible little poodle, Felix, and frequents an artificial sort of worship under a 'phoney' clergyman, Father Benger.

'Dulcie felt a sense of unreality coming over her, as she often did when in conversation with her neighbours. It was one of their chief charms, their being so out of touch with everyday life and reminding her of England in the twenties or São Paulo in the nineties.' A critic tells us that Senhor MacBride Pereira illustrates 'some of the difficulties encountered by the stranger in an alien culture', and says that he is 'hopelessly confused by what he sees'. He seems to me more like those 'untrained Observers' who are 'subjective cameras, each with his or her own distortion. They tell us not what society is like but what it looks like to them.' It looks as if, on her own (as anyone easily could), Barbara has hit on the Mass Observation formula (which I do not think she had anywhere seen). Thus read, his 'observations' are haphazard, but not nonsensical.

> 'A young English girl with a pot plant – what could be more charming?'
> 'The things I see! ... Who knows what it might not be?'

He does not know, but he knows what he sees.

Moreover he gives us a little information about 'collective habits and social behaviour' in his own country. 'In Latin America, and especially in Brazil, it is *not* considered nice for a man to go to church.'

It is not until *A Few Green Leaves* that Barbara's intention was ever mainly anthropological. Emma is there described as 'an anthropologist and observer', but I hardly think there is a conscious distinction between these two complementary functions. Though Emma is mainly interested in 'collective habits and social behaviour', as an anthropologist, she has an 'observer's' passionate concern for unconsidered trifles, and has certainly no wish to influence behaviour. The 'observers' in the 'canon' are almost purely observers.

In *No Fond Return* there are perhaps rather too many subjective cameras clicking away; they produce a great richness of detail, but there is not a strong enough central interest to give it sufficient coherence.

[9]

An Unsuitable Attachment

This novel, offered by Barbara to Cape in 1963, was rejected, and thus began her long period of silence.

Mr Philip Larkin, in his foreword to the publication in 1982, reasonably expresses surprise that a blank rejection should have been given by this firm to an author for whom they had published six novels that had been well received. It would have been proper to invite Barbara to talk it over, and perhaps to offer suggestions for the improvement of her book. However, Jonathan Cape was now dead, and perhaps it was he who had been most favourably inclined towards her former novels. Moreover it is difficult to see what suggestions could have been offered.

Like a more celebrated work, *Northanger Abbey*, which also came out after its author's death, it seems to have a fatal flaw in its structure. We are glad to have these books for the sake of many felicities in them, but it is difficult to see how their authors could have brought them into a form satisfying to themselves, and the authors evidently could not see this either. It is not surprising that Cape's readers gave this book negative reports.

My own belief is that a good book could have been made – not out the novel itself, but out of some of its characters and incidents employed in a different plot, in which the 'attachment' might have been scrapped or minimized. I shall adopt a presumptuous form of criticism which, had I had the chance, I would have discussed with Barbara herself – for only her invention could have supplied the necessary additions.

There are several characters asking for development and needing a story of their own in which to show their paces. These are the Revd Mark Ainger and Sophia his wife, and two newly come residents in their North London parish, Rupert Stonebird and Ianthe Broome. Probably one or more important new characters could have been brought in to join them as part of the 'subject'. The light *ficelles* (as Henry James calls them) who belong not to the 'subject' of the novel but to the 'treatment' are not lacking as 'provision for the reader's amusement'.*

Barbara would, I feel sure, have found as much story as she needed simply by listening (as Gide did) to her characters talking, and by looking at them as Turgeniev looked at his: trying to reconstruct a *dossier* of their previous lives, feeling that such people must do something very special and interesting.

The most suggestive passage in the novel, from this point of view, is a brief conversation between Rupert and Ianthe.

'I feel Sophia knows about life.' Rupert went on.

'You mean living in this poor parish and being married to a clergyman – yes, I suppose she would know about life.'

'Yes, that would be the conventional view of course – that a woman in those circumstances would know about life, but I meant something a little different.... Something that the pessimistic Victorians had, not the women, the men. I was thinking of Matthew Arnold.'

'Oh?'...

'I think she sometimes feels that there really is neither joy nor love, nor light....'

Here we have important information about two or even three of the characters. Rupert is seen to be particularly perceptive, and he has told us something about Sophia which we had not before

*Robert Liddell, *A Treatise on the Novel*, Jonathan Cape, London, 1947, p. 90 and idem, *Some Principles of Fiction*, Jonathan Cape, London, 1953, p. 101.

known but which we feel to be certainly true. He seems to find
Ianthe's reactions rather crass.

At once she gives herself away. '"I don't think one should feel
like that about life," said Ianthe, a little shocked. "A clergyman's
wife shouldn't anyway."'

But we had already suspected that she was a prig.

Emphasis is given in this passage to two themes only lightly
indicated in the book: themes which Barbara has not elsewhere
treated in the 'canon', though they must have been well within her
range as they cannot have been outside her experience and
observation. There is the friendship between Rupert and Sophia,
an unromantic relationship between a man and a woman more
profound than that between Mildred and Julian – for whom an
'excellent woman must be, among other things, an additional
curate' (*EW*). If this were further developed one cannot believe
that Sophia would use Rupert so ill as to wish her silly young sister
on to him. The other theme is the dislike of one woman for another
(of Ianthe for Sophia), a pure antipathy, not due to any rivalry
emotional or professional. In a confined world, like St Basil's
parish, both may be rich in developments.

Father Ainger, Mark, is the vicar of St Basil's, a hideous Gothic
revival church in a North London parish. He comes of a good
clerical family, but is conscious of his lack of private means. He is
extremely detached from the world, dryer than Julian Malory
(*EW*). He is a forceful preacher, with a habit of beginning his
sermons with an arresting image, asking his hearers to imagine
themselves gazing at the pyramids or the New York skyline – one
can hardly suppose that he himself ever enjoyed such an
experience, though we know that he has visited Italy. A casual
encounter with the vicar of St Mary's, Pimlico (is this still Julian?)
makes Ianthe compare him unfavourably with Mark. She had
judged that vicar 'to be one of those unfortunate men who dislike
their neighbours more than they dislike themselves.... How
much nicer Mark Ainger was, assuming in his remote kindness that
everybody knew about the things he was interested in himself and

being much too charitable to pass judgement on other people's amusements, however unlike his own though they might be.' But Ianthe is not a very competent witness.

Celibacy, of course, makes a difference: Julian is more pestered by 'excellent women', whether or not their interests are matrimonial; and his sister does not make much of a home for him.

Mark is married to Sophia and devoted to her, and she divides her devotion between him and her cat, Faustina – who gets the larger share. Faustina had had 'the operation', and might have been expected to settle down cosily to being an 'excellent cat', but she was allowed to dominate the household and to impose her temperamental vagaries as well as her physical needs – for Sophia thinks Mark comfortably free from the former.

'I feel sometimes that I can't reach Faustina as I've reached other cats. And somehow it's the same with Mark,' she tells Ianthe, who is shocked again – she has no sense of humour.

Walking down the Spanish Steps, during their excursion to Rome, Mark feels for a moment that Sophia is all his, without Faustina. He generously wonders what Faustina is doing.

'I don't know,' says Sophia. 'She's so unpredictable. Perhaps she's even giving to someone else the love and devotion she's never given to me.'

Often fanatical cat-lovers seem to want quantity rather than quality in their pets, but Sophia (like Dr Johnson) attended to her cat's feelings, and would not make Faustina jealous by giving her a companion.

Faustina is delightfully funny, with anything from a palm cross to a lobster patty in her mouth; and she is very beautiful – tortoiseshell with a creamy underside, and a gold streak on her dark head. She is not the less sympathetic because of Ianthe's priggishness, or Sister Dew's impertinently patronizing remarks about 'Pussy'. Rupert Stonebird, more sensitive, remembers not to refer to her as 'it'.

'She's all I've got,' says Sophia – and one wonders whether we really ought to smile – ought we not rather to think of Matthew

Arnold's 'darkling plain' and Sophia alone on it, but for a cat quite indifferent to her feelings? If Sophia had said: 'Ah love, let us be true to one another', she might have received a dusty answer, a cynical 'miaow'.

Sophia's mother, Mrs Grandison, sends her quinces from a more gracious house redolent of well-polished furniture and Earl Grey tea. The vicarage had been built to match the church, 'and the style of the rooms had not yet and perhaps never would become fashionable again'. But Sophia does not repine – though Mark has refused a smart London church, St Ermin's. She has her Earl Grey tea, and makes quince jelly. Sometimes as she walks about her drab neighbourhood she plays a game with herself, imagining that she is in Italy – of which she has some knowledge.

Her young sister Penelope works for a London publisher and, aged twenty-five, is passionately anxious to marry. Sophia wishes to help her, as Jane (*JP*) wished to help Prudence; but she is full of intrigues and tortuous imaginings. She is far more highly strung than Jane, in fact the character in the 'canon' who is nearest to being tragic – as Jane, perhaps, is the furthest from it. Her analogies are even more exuberant and wilder than Jane's, but as a 'clergy wife' she is less tactless and clumsy – and a far better cook.

The arrival of another gentlewoman in the parish, Ianthe Broome, is a great pleasure to her, as she has missed contact with people of her own kind. It was with a mild surprise that, near the end of the book, she began to realize that Ianthe did not like her.

Rupert Stonebird is a lecturer on social anthropology in London. A man of thirty-six, 'not yet married' – which seems to imply that marriage is a fate that will ultimately befall him. A clergyman's son, he had suddenly regained his faith after years of agnosticism and, of all times and places, it had happened when he had 'popped in' out of curiosity to solemn evensong at St Basil's. Another gentleman in the parish could hardly escape Sophia's attention – she at once decided that he was to marry her sister and almost rudely kept him away from Ianthe. He was a quiet man, who liked observing without being observed. His conscience, which had been for a long time silent, was now continually nagging him and obliging him to unnecessary and uncongenial parochial and social activities, and the neighbourhood was only too glad to swallow him up. He was mildly attracted by Ianthe. 'A vague idea formed in his mind – not that he loved her, but that he would like to see her always in his house, like some suitable decoration or finishing touch.' Later he came to find her even more 'suitable', not improbably in contrast with silly young Penelope (whom he called a 'Pre-Raphaelite beatnik') whose clothes – whether tartan trews or silver lamé – were put on without thought of fashion, but simply to attract attention; Ianthe might have had the opposite purpose always in mind.

He is not unimaginative; when he sees Ianthe to her door for the first time he remarks that she has left a light on in the hall. She explains:

'I feel it discourages burglars, and it seems more welcoming when one comes back to an empty house.'

Oh, this coming back to an empty house, Rupert thought, when he had seen her safely up to her door. People – though perhaps it was only women – seemed to make so much of it. As if life itself were not as empty as the house one was coming back to.

He did not go on, as 'people' usually do not, to imagine the bliss of coming back to an empty house when we have endured a turbulent family life, or any prolonged period of institutional existence – then the empty house can be our fortress and our ease.

He has shown sensitiveness about Sophia, and is far too good for Penelope; we may come to wonder if Ianthe is good enough for him.

The first impression given by Ianthe Broome is excellent; she is a canon's daughter, the only child of elderly parents, and has lived too long in a small flat with her widowed mother. She is tall and fragile-looking, with a kind of unsmart elegance about her – not at all well placed as an assistant in a library of political and sociological books, where so many of the readers are 'ill-mannered, grubby students and cranks of all ages'. Like Mildred, another clergyman's daughter, she has inherited some good furniture: some Hepplewhite chairs and a Pembroke table. Her boss at the library wants to marry her for them.

Unfortunately a new junior assistant joins the library, to whom Ianthe forms an 'unsuitable attachment'. She was every inch a gentlewoman (if rather bourgeoise), who wore 'ladylike stockings with seams' and 'brown court shoes of good leather with a sensible heel'; but John Challow was not quite a gentleman: 'his shoes seemed to be a little too pointed – not quite what men one knew would wear'. But as Ianthe had no social position to keep up and no family to raise objections – apart from an uncle and aunt – this sort of unsuitability does not seem to matter to anyone else. As Sophia says (speaking generally): 'Perhaps it doesn't concern anybody but the woman herself – obviously it doesn't. *She* is the one who must know in her heart whether he is suitable or not, whatever other people may think.' It is for *her* to decide if too great an irritation may be caused by differences of accent or manners.

That might be all very well if only a brief affair were in question, or if only social unsuitability were the impediment – if, for example, the couple were united by a common interest, such as anthropology. But when Sophia has to speak to Ianthe's uncle and aunt she seems to know more about John's intellectual and moral inferiority (we are not told how she has come to know this). 'There is the rest of their lives,' she says, 'and marriage is for a long time. What will they talk about in the evenings when the novelty has worn off?' But Ianthe's uncle and aunt dismiss the evenings: 'the man can go to his club while the woman watches television'. Perhaps they will give her a television set for a wedding present.

Ianthe herself, before things had gone so far, began wondering about John. 'Would it be possible to go round sight-seeing with him and expect him to say the sort of thing appropriate to the occasion? But perhaps if they were to have any kind of life

[95]

together, none of it – or very little – would be spent in looking at churches and picture galleries so it wouldn't matter. Plenty of people did without that sort of thing and were perfectly happy. . . .' She did not see that marriage with John would mean intellectual and spiritual impoverishment, such as that which Viola Dace (*NFR*) so cheerfully accepted; and we rather despise her for contemplating such an abdication. Thinking back we see how priggish and schoolmistressy she is capable of being, though she looks above it.

Mervyn, who employs both John and Ianthe, points out to her that when she is forty John will still be in his thirties. He does not need to develop the implications. John's attempts at courting are not engaging. He borrows money from Ianthe, and it is a disappointment to the reader that he ultimately pays it back. It would have been much better if Barbara had kept to her original plan: 'John had been meant to be much worse',* and Ianthe a victim. It is not recorded why Barbara changed her mind. John might have got money out of Ianthe, and there might even have been an attempted seduction. It must, of course, be unsuccessful, but it could go far enough to shock Ianthe without shocking the reader.

He kisses her at a station barrier, and she goes off on the parish excursion to Rome with that memory; in Rome, among the azaleas on the Spanish Steps, she is sure that she is in love with him. She 'lets love sweep over her like a kind of illness'; and no good can come of it.

There had been a moment when Ianthe had deliberately tried to turn her thoughts away from John and towards Rupert Stonebird, who also wished to marry her. If the attachment to John were broken, perhaps painfully, Ianthe might gain weight morally and intellectually, and be more worthy of Rupert. She has not yet, it would seem, suffered any important experience. She is so easily shocked – too easily for a woman of her generation – that one

A Very Private Eye, p. 222.

cannot feel she is so much 'a lady' as Sophia, or even so 'Catholic' (despite her father s photograph in a biretta).

Perhaps Barbara was afraid of repeating the end of *Excellent Women*, where Mildred is beginning a closer friendship with Everard who (like Rupert) is an excellent churchman and a convert, as well as being a cultured gentleman and an anthropologist. She could have done more to individualize Rupert or have introduced an entirely new character. But Ianthe's marriage need not be a central interest – and an approach to Rupert, which need not have led so far, could have produced 'unpleasantness' with Sophia, who regards Ianthe as a friend but intends Rupert for Penelope. An easy solution would be to dispose of Penelope.

However, the wedding takes place. One might ask Ianthe, who mentally criticized Sophia for comparing 'a sacred and honourable estate like marriage to a relationship with a cat', how she could enter into such an estate with John because love had 'swept over' her, like influenza. Lady Chatterley must soon have tired of her lover, and E.M. Forster's friends were not prepared to give the lovers in *Maurice* more than a few weeks together. These couples, it is true, had not been united by the Church or the Law, but one may expect that the sacramental and legal benison will only serve as tiresome impediments when Ianthe needs to get free again or has been abandoned. Sophia and Rupert are sad and angry. One of the officiating clergy remarks that we may now think of the Challows 'Imparadised in one another's arms as Milton put it ... or encasseroled perhaps.'

This might pass if Ianthe were not meant to be an important character – the sad wedding could then be an end-of-the-book reception for other characters, like the end of *STG*. It will not do here, and certainly is not fit to give a title to the book.

[10]

A Summing-up

It was fortunate for Barbara that *An Unsuitable Attachment* was not published, even in a revised state. It would certainly have attracted unfavourable notices, and might probably have been followed by another book written from the declining impulse of the 'canon', and then a final rejection. After that the author might not unreasonably have thought that she had 'written herself out', and her silence might thenceforth have been unbroken. The Second Period was the result of the refusal, and Barbara could have quoted (and very likely did quote) from her favourite hymn: 'The Bud May Have a Bitter Taste, But Sweet Will Be the Flower'.

The 'canon' remains, unspoilt by the last failure, and can thus be estimated. The cast is limited, no one is really evil – with the possible exception of Allegra Gray – no one is worse than unthinkingly selfish, no one is very unkind or deceitful or savage. There is none of the cruelty, tyranny or deep hypocrisy that are rife in the novels of Ivy Compton-Burnett. There is no violence: the two violent deaths (of John Akenside and Tom) are reported from 'abroad' and far away: only old Mrs Beamish dies on the spot, and not unexpectedly. There is never any 'conflict' of duties', and no temptation accepted or resisted (George Eliot's speciality). We do not hear of any of her characters going to confession, though we know that at Christmas Father Thames was hearing confessions for hours behind the purple brocade curtains of his confessional. Money is less important than in most 'domestic' English novels. In

'Pymdom' everyone that matters has enough to stave off want or anxiety, but not enough to provoke envy or to invite to a change of life. We do not know (though Jane Austen would have told us) how much they have. I do not think this is due to the author's 'shyness' on the subject, but more to the fluctuation of money values in our time. The only financial interest is in the 'grants' for field work given to some of the anthropologists.

The turning event is usually the entry of a new character into a small world or a confined life. The Napiers come into the flat below Mildred, and Allegra rents the upper floor of the vicarage (*EW*). Jane, herself the heroine, comes into the new world of a country parish (*JP*). Wilmet makes the acquaintance of Father Thames (she is not really his parishioner) and renews her acquaintance with Piers (*GB*). Dulcie goes away to a conference and meets Viola Dace and Aylwin Forbes, and later takes them into her life (*NFR*). Sophia Ainger reflects that 'there was always that slight excitement about living in a London parish – one never knew who might turn up in church on Sunday' – and several new people came into her life (*UA*).

The same pattern is, in one way or another, always discernible in Jane Austen's novels, and there again is the harmony or discord arising from the absorption of new life, and the continuation of the old. Ivy Compton-Burnett sometimes uses a similar design, but her families or schools generally have their own virus within them from the start. Dame Ivy, like Jane Austen, sometimes allows Death to intervene, and like George Eliot she permits violence.

Any analysis of this kind omits or bypasses what is really important, the quality of thought and feeling which informs the books – hence the worthlessness of many academic theses, and hence the tiresome obligation on the critic to tell much of the story, and to let the author speak for herself or through the mouths of her characters as much as possible – and the speeches require much of the story to be told, to provide the necessary context. If we say (for example) that Jane Austen has nearly always a 'Cinderella' theme, that George Eliot is usually concerned with a moral choice, that Ivy Compton-Burnett exposes the abuse of power, and that Barbara usually offers a muted love-story, we have said very little.

To the first five sections concerned with the 'canon' I have given the title of some of Barbara's varied interests. 'The Kitchen Sink' dominated the life of Mildred (*EW*) and what seems to have been the author's favourite novel. 'Village and Office' are two lives that she knew much about (*JP*), though the office seems to have bored her. 'The Anthropologists' form a 'kind of chorus to the stories of Catherine and Deirdre. Barbara makes a happy use of her experience as editor of *Africa*, and is quite ready to admit that that continent has not really much benefited from anthropology. 'The Clergy House' is the centre of the next novel. The other main theme, the heroine's vain pursuit of the wrong sort of man, will be further developed with deeper feeling in the next period. It is almost prophetic; life does indeed seem to imitate art, perhaps because the artist has been able to express tendencies that he has not yet had the opportunity to fulfil in life. 'Investigation', almost prying into other people's lives in an innocent way, had long been a hobby of Barbara's: even an unusual notice in the personal column of a newspaper could arouse her curiosity, and a curiosity that demanded fulfilment. *No Fond Return of Love* is her own sort of detective story.

A further reason for the failure of *An Unsuitable Attachment* may be that it does not dramatize any of the author's particular interests.

A feature in the 'canon' that I think hardly survives into the Second Period may be called fantasy or 'play'; the characters often play a sort of intellectual game with others or by themselves. Two of the novels, the first and last of the 'canon' (*STG* and *NFR*), are almost all play. The first novel began that way, Barbara imagining herself and her friends as thirty years older. The last is Dulcie Mainwaring's form of detective story. Jane's extraordinary malapropisms, odd quotations and non sequiturs are also part of a life of fantasy. For example, there is her care that a neighbouring clergyman should not arrive at supper-time and see them eating liver (as in the years of post-war austerity he would not have had any). 'He had better not see us eating it. Like meat offered to idols.... You will remember St Paul had no objection to the faithful eating it, but pointed out that it might prove a stumbling block to the weaker brethren – not that Father Lomax would be that of course' (*JP*).

'Playfulness' is not generally a word of approval; it often suggests archness, and once or twice heroines fall into this. If they do, Barbara provides a man at hand to restrain them. Catherine and Tom were walking down a suburban road (*LA*):

> She was in what he thought of as one of her worst moods this afternoon, the kind he found most difficult to cope with. The less encouragement he gave her, the more wild and frivolous would her fancies become. Now, to this horror, she began to sing, something about lotus flowers and finding Nirvana within his loving arms.
>
> > *'As the river flows to the ocean,*
> > *My soul, my soul shall flow to thine!'*

Poor Catherine, the 'trite little stories' that she had to produce for glossy magazines for women, generally with happy endings, were no outlet to the more vigorous part of her mind and feelings. She seemed to have an individual mental kaleidoscope, composed of bits of Shakespeare's sonnets and popular songs, among other scraps – and to turn it without rhyme or reason.

Wilmet, walking in the park, meets Piers, apparently absorbed in a border of lupins (*GB*). She says, gushingly, that she would like to get in among them and smell their peppery smell.

Piers tells her to be cool and dignified, and to behave in character, 'not plunging in among lupins'.

She complains that this 'doesn't sound very lovable'.

'Wilmet, what's the matter with you? You're talking like one of the cheaper women's magazines.' Piers' tone was rather petulant.

'Love is the cheapest of all emotions,' I thought; or such a universal one that it makes one talk like a cheap magazine.

Mildred and Wilmet, the two narrators, are somewhat restrained by their function – and Mildred is so observant that she hardly needs to invent. But they are both 'churchy', and as Anglo-Catholics of a happy period,* 'They play the Lambeth way.' There are always little fantasies and humours in church life, and the delightful church newspaper had idiosyncratic answers to correspondents. Barbara might well have parodied it more than twice.

Sophia, too good for her North London parish – and too good for the novel in which she is placed (*UA*) – when she walked about her dingy neighbourhood liked to imagine herself in Italy, not necessarily in a beautiful or famous part, 'but perhaps in some obscure little town in the Alban hills'.

Nor is 'play' or fantasy confined to women. It redeems the only men in the 'canon' who can be called attractive – that is to say attractive to the reader who cannot see, and is therefore unmoved by the vulgar good looks of John Challow or the 'pretty faces' of Aylwin and Neville Forbes. Tom (*LA*) and Piers (*GB*) are also personable. The first is loved by three women, not entirely satisfactorily, the second by one without response. They are *déclassés* and dissatisfied; one is heterosexual, the other homosexual, and it is a proof of Barbara's knowledge of human nature that they are so very alike in other ways, despite their different circumstances. They have some sardonic humour, are cruel to friends of their own size but kind to adolescents (Deirdre and Keith). They would (no doubt) be kind to animals. Readers who are often masochistic, and still more often adolescent, may like them better than they deserve.

*Of whom I speak only with love and respect.

The only really attractive men have a tendency to 'play' or fantasy. Rocky Napier and Father Marius Ransome thus amuse the narrators, Mildred and Wilmet. Jean Pierre le Rossignol (*LA*) is of course only playing at an anthropological study of the English, who find him entertaining and charming. Old Felix Mainwaring indulges himself with the most elaborate fantasy, inviting four students to spend a weekend at his country house in order that he may study their manners and reactions in the way in which candidates for the Foreign Service are legendarily believed to have been tested.

One form of 'play' is a little tiresome. 'Analogies' of one sort or another may be amusing in pencil and paper games, but will seldom please if they appear, somewhat laboured, at any length in the cold print of fiction. Wilmet, for example, 'wondered if there were perhaps some special kind of meal provided (at a reduced price) for women whose escorts had failed to turn up'. To pass the time she amused herself 'by composing the menu' (*GB*). But it does not much amuse the reader.

The men, if not 'playful', are generally rather dull; they are often just 'husband-types', consorts in fact, unless they are distinguished into various kinds of clergymen, whether celibate or not. The dull women would be dull indeed if one had to meet them or their like in real life, but in the 'canon' each has her useful place to set off the heroine. Viola Dace, by contrast, makes us esteem Dulcie, who is simple and modest where Viola is pretentious: one feels that Viola has strayed into the chaste 'canon' from a novel by another author who would have allowed her more love-life – here she has too little to do. Ianthe (*UA*), a dreary prig, is wrongly cast as a leading lady, and dislikes Sophia, who thoroughly deserves that role. Deirdre is an almost equally watery young woman, but the interest of that book (*LA*) rests firmly on Catherine. Mary Beamish is the most useful of the minor woman characters. She not only points a moral – she contributes to Wilmet's partial regeneration – she also adorns the tale. She alone marries a desirable husband, as she deserves (*GB*).

[103]

Older women seem better able to retain and exhibit their individuality. Deirdre's aunt, Rhoda Wellcome, and her mother, Mrs Swan, with their little tussles over household detail, are far more engaging than Deirdre (*LA*). Miss Prideaux (*GB*) who has been a governess in foreign parts, in royal and imperial families, recalls past splendours. 'Two litres of Chianti *from our own vineyards* was sent up to the schoolroom *every day*.' She was 'of the generation which wears a hat in the house for luncheon and tea', and entertained people to tea in 'her little drawing-room as she called it, which was really a bed-sitting-room in the flat of some other people' – but her guests included an ex-ambassador and there were silver-framed photographs of minor European royalties.

Sophia's mother (*UA*) had a house redolent of bowls of quinces, the fragrance of well-polished furniture and good China tea – much of which Sophia could not adequately reproduce in North London. Mrs Grandison, coming with the stingy Lady Selvedge (the 'relict not widow' of Sir Humphrey), whom she has persuaded to open her daughter's bazaar, is obliged by the latter to eat a three-and-ninepenny luncheon in a snack bar on the way, instead of 'a cut off splendid classic sirloin' or 'sole in an exquisite sauce'. Lady Selvedge is equally mean about transport and denies them a taxi; but Mrs Grandison was wearing light shoes while Lady Selvedge had 'low-heeled walking shoes, not really quite the thing with her elaborately draped velvet toque but eminently suitable'.

The writing is simple, and appears unstudied, though it has usually been revised with care. It is generally concrete, going into considerable detail, and we are well aware of what the people eat and what clothes they wear. This helps to create the world that is Barbara's achievement. We also know a great deal about the furnishing of their houses: the 'good pieces' owned by Mildred and Rocky (*EW*), by Ianthe and, surprisingly, by Miss Grimes (*UA*); the pleasant 'Bohemian' effect of Catherine's underfurnished living-room, the chintzy cosiness of Deirdre's home (*LA*); the Clevelands' chilly curtains that did not quite meet, and the Regency discomfort of Prudence's flat (*JP*). Everything is observed, but not tiresomely overdescribed, and the flow of the books is easy. And then one is suddenly held up by the thoughts of one of the characters, whether they have passed into spoken words or not. There is often a pleasant 'dottiness' (it is hard to find a better word) about a simile joined on to an idea or image coming directly from household cares, most often connected with food. This 'yoking together of heterogeneous ideas' may owe something to Barbara's love of metaphysical poetry.

Of young people: 'They talked so glibly about divorce and remarriage, as if it were nothing more complicated than mincing the cold beef and making it into a shepherd's pie.'

Of widows: '"They have a knack of catching a man. Having done it once they can do it again. I suppose there is nothing in it when you know how." "Like mending a flue."' Or: 'Widows always do marry again . . . or they very often do. It must be strange to replace somebody like that, though I suppose one doesn't actually replace them, I mean not in the way you buy a new teapot when the old one is broken.'

Of faith: Jane Cleveland is bottling plums. 'It seems to require such a very great deal of faith to lift them just by their glass tops. I suppose it's like going over to Rome – once you see that it works you wonder you could ever have doubted it.' Or: 'I somehow felt the cold weather might discourage doubts, or at least temporarily suspend intellectual activity, like food preserved by freezing.'

In all these there is a startling but admirable lack of 'the dissociation of sensibility'.

There are flashes of quite ordinary common sense, which are oddly comical in their context. Dulcie thinks: 'it was almost within walking distance if one were wearing comfortable shoes'.* Wilmet, feeling sorry that Father Bode never received invitations to luncheon like Father Thames, thought: 'I was sure that Father Bode was equally worthy of eating smoked salmon and grouse or

---

*I hope (but without much confidence) that no imbecile will write a psychoanalytic article on 'Barbara Pym and Shoes'.

whatever luncheon the hostesses might care to provide. Then it occurred to me that he might well be the kind of person who would prefer tinned salmon, though I was ashamed of the unworthy thought for I knew him to be a good man.'

Two of the similes I find incomprehensible. The rabbit produced by a conjurer from nothing at a children's party may stand for surprise, but does not justify an unexpected declaration of love as being 'like having a large white rabbit thrust into your arms, and not knowing what to do with it'. 'If you don't see, I can't explain,' said Mildred (*EW*) who has used this image. We may leave it like that.

Dulcie (*NFR*) we are told 'thought confusedly' when, considering her broken engagement, she reflected: 'Perhaps it is sadder to have loved somebody "unworthy", and the end of it is such a very little thing, like a child's coffin.' This is puzzling, and perhaps not very well expressed, but Dulcie was 'confused'.

The successful novels owe their cohesion to their heroines, to Mildred, Jane and Prudence, Catherine and Wilmet – Dulcie is not quite strong enough to hold her novel together. *An Unsuitable Attachment*, if published when it was intended, would have been a miserable afterpiece. Its fate (we can now see) ought to have been very different – instead of standing at the end of the 'canon', with a heroine duller than Viola Dace or Deirdre, it ought (in a very thoroughly revised and altered form, and perhaps after two or three years of silence) to have appeared as the first novel of the Second Period, with Sophia as heroine. Ianthe, if she still were allowed a place, ought to be well in the background. John, unless he were really made much 'worse' than anyone in the 'canon', ought to have been jettisoned, shoes and all.

THREE

The Later Years

11

The Sweet Dove Died

Although Barbara's time in the wilderness after the rejection of a manuscript in 1963 was not over until January 1977, when Philip Larkin and Lord David Cecil named her in *The Times Literary Supplement* as one of the most underrated writers of the century, she had not stopped writing, and had two new novels ready to offer for publication – indeed they had both been rejected before she was thus restored to the notice of the literary world.

She had wasted (as it seems to me) a good deal of time revising *An Unsuitable Attachment*, whereas the better things in it needed to be set in a better story. But in 1963 she was already taking notes that were to come to life in *The Sweet Dove Died*.

On 15 August 1963 she wrote: 'Walking in Bond Street, I see a young man sitting alone in a grand antique shop, presumably waiting for customers. A woman admirer might be a great nuisance always coming to see him.' This may be an early inspiration for James Boyce. By 1968 she had completed a draft of the book, 'in the main', about 'the relationship of an older woman with a younger man'.

The 'younger man' was unlike Richard Roberts, a charming Bahamian whom she had already met in 1961, and who dealt in antiques. Barbara's editors say that the book was 'inspired, in part' by her affection for him. *In part* should be italicized. Certainly she took more interest than before in porcelain, etc., and once or twice she attended book sales on Richard's behalf; these new interests contributed to her story – but she has not written an *Old Curiosity Shop*. On the personal level, he seems to have appreciated her, and it is not recorded why their friendship – as friendships will – dried up. I shall not commit the impertinence of trying to construct any story from the novel and from Barbara's papers.

This novel, the last book to appear in the author's lifetime, though published in 1978 after *Quartet in Autumn*, was in fact written earlier, and for that reason I deal with it here, and also because it forms a bridge between the 'canon' and the second period. It has at bottom the same 'muted love-story', though with a difference. The heroine is middle-aged, just under fifty, and gradually falls in love with a basically homosexual man half her age, beginning as his Egeria. As such he is much attached to her, until she tires him out by her attentions and possessiveness – and his male lover deals the final blow to their friendship.

This book is deeper and darker than the 'canon'. I suspect that Barbara was getting tired of writing cosy books which offer so much repose and relaxation to the reader – and tired perhaps of her readers' appreciation. Did she say to herself: 'I want to be a real novelist'? I do not know, and hope that she did not undervalue the 'canon', though she may well have felt that it was time for her to do something else. She wrote to Philip Larkin that she 'intended to leave out boring cosiness and concentrate on the darker side', and again that she 'ruthlessly suppressed (or tried to) all "cosiness"'* – although the 'cosiest' page in this book is perhaps the only one that fulfils Ste Beuve's demand for a glimpse of 'desirable life'. She also pared away the ecclesiastical and anthropological references of the 'canon', and only once allowed a character from a former book to visit us in this.

Only once did she play her game of analogies: '"A little china castle and that was cracked" A bit like Phoebe, perhaps. What was Leonora like? A piece of Meissen without flaw? It would be an amusing game to liken one's friends and acquaintances to

A Very Private Eye, pp. 244 and 251.

antiques.' It would not be very amusing.

Only once is a minor character allowed the free play of a Jane Cleveland.

'I think Miss Eyre took it, Miss,' said the man at the furniture depository.

'*Jane* Eyre?' asked Jennifer. 'I don't like the sound of *that*.'

'Miss Leonora Eyre,' said the man....

'Those Leonora overtures,' went on Jennifer gaily. 'I never did like Beethoven. The mixture of that and Jane Eyre is rather *disquieting*, don't you think?'

Jennifer has strayed out of the 'canon'.

Leonora Eyre, the heroine, is certainly not like Barbara. She is less cultured (at all events, less literary) and, as heroines in fiction often are, is in some ways more fortunate than her creator. She has been left well enough off to have no need to work, and she has part of a pretty house, and a collection of small Victorian objects. She has the time and the means to be elegant – an elegance that she wishes to carry into every part of her life. She 'liked to think of her life as calm of mind, all passion spent, or more rarely as emotion recollected in tranquillity. But had there really been emotion? One or two tearful scenes in bed – for she had never enjoyed *that* kind of thing – and it was such a relief that she didn't have to worry any more.' She is like a middle-aged actress (in another woman's novel) who is thankful that she will never again have to be 'half a brace of lovers' on the stage. Thus far she is a true Pym heroine, ready for a 'muted love-story', and emotionally she has much in common with Mildred or Dulcie – though she would think herself, and would generally be thought their social superior. Indeed in the novels of the second period Barbara seems to enlarge her social range; both belong to the middle class, but in *The Sweet Dove* the *milieu* is generally higher socially than in the 'canon', and in *Quartet* it is lower. In both of them an outer world is more felt.

Leonora is all that is moderate: elegant but not smart, good-looking but not beautiful, intelligent but not an intellectual, a gentlewoman but not aristocratic, comfortably off but not rich, consular not ambassadorial. Her father's consular post has made her something of a bore; her friends and acquaintances avoid mentioning such names as Vienna, Lisbon or Dresden for fear of provoking a spate of reminiscences. Pym characters seem always to have photographs in their bedrooms, even when they stay in hotels or other people's houses; Leonora has set up her grandparents as looking more distinguished than her father and mother, though no eyes but her own are likely to see them.

She 'had never been badly treated or rejected by a man – perhaps she had never loved another person with enough intensity for such a thing to be possible'. But she tried to be comforting to those who were unhappy. On one such occasion she 'felt she had done some good, an unusual sensation to her and one she rather liked'. She had no religion, but liked to be able to admire her image of herself. 'One tries to lead a good life . . . one enjoys the arts and gives something to charity of course and . . . one loves people to the best of one's ability.' On the whole she is cautious – unlike Barbara, far less warm-hearted and generous, and entirely without her sense of humour. The most we can conjecture is that Barbara may sometimes have wished to be a little more like Leonora – and happily she was not.

Leonora's women friends are not impressive, and she did not much care to cultivate them, though their unhappiness made her own life still more desirable by contrast. Liz bred beautiful but hideously screaming Siamese cats, to fill her life now that she had had to get rid of her brute of a husband. They certainly kept her busy and uneasy. Meg, left over from the time when Leonora had a job, had a protégé, a pretty, fragile young man called Colin, who had a series of lovers – 'a young man in advertising, a television producer, a civil servant, an Indian, even a curate' – for whose ill-usage Meg had to console him. When he disappeared for some weeks Meg went tearfully to Leonora for comfort. 'He's all I've got.'

We may be reminded (as the first readers could not have been, for the book was not yet published) of Sophia and her cat Faustina (*UA*). Sophia, an intelligent and religious woman, could probably have faced the 'darkling plain' of life with no other support. Colin would have been of less use than the cat. Meg ought to have bought herself a nice spaniel, or *one* of Liz's Siamese.

Leonora was satisfied that her own life was much better balanced and more fortunate. But her defences had been pierced. One of the morals to be drawn from this book – and there are several – is that pride goes before a fall.

Overcome by the heat, she collapsed at an auction sale, and was picked up by Humphrey Boyce (aged fifty-nine) and James Boyce (twenty-four) his nephew, and his assistant in an antique shop. Humphrey, a widower of some years' standing, seemed to be interested in Miss Eyre, and James thought she would be a suitable second wife for his uncle. However, from the first, Leonora was more interested in James, who was strikingly good-looking. 'One needed the company of young people sometimes,' she thought. One may ask, 'Why?' But it is a give-away remark that people often make without thinking. At their second meeting she invited him into her house, and gave him an impromptu meal. 'One always has *something* – tins and packets and eggs and things in the fridge.' One wonders for what eventuality she is so fully provided.

Her friendship with uncle and nephew continued. Little did she know that on an afternoon when Humphrey had motored her to Virginia Water, James was having a secret adventure.

A note of Barbara's is rather puzzling: 'Blurb for my nearly finished novel. What is it about? The struggle of two women, unknown to each other, to get a young man who doesn't want either of them.'*

This is not what the finished novel is about.

James has encountered a tall, plain girl, Phoebe Sharpe, at a party; neither of them seemed to know anyone there, and they

*Cited in *The Pleasure of Miss Pym*, p. 49.

were hedged into a corner by other people. She was shy, and was surprised that he did not try to talk to prettier girls, but girlish prettiness was of no interest to him, and anyway they could hardly escape from each other. He took her out to dinner and learned that she was living in a cottage in the country, and editing the literary remains of a dead girl, Anthea Wedge (another example of Barbara's skill in naming characters, on which John Betjeman remarked once in a review), for publication in a slim volume by her bereaved parents.

Finding himself at an auction to which Humphrey had sent him in the same village, James called on Phoebe, who surprisingly and swiftly seduced him. James hardly understood how it had happened, but was not displeased to find he had another accomplishment. However, he did not wish for an entanglement, and it was very imprudent of him to offer to lend her some furniture during a tour that he was shortly going to make of Spain and Portugal, to pick up what he could for Humphrey's shop. Unfortunately he mentioned a fruitwood mirror, of which Leonora was fond. But Phoebe was never important to him, and she never struggled to 'get' James. She had read English literature at an obscure university, and perhaps had more culture and imagination than James or Leonora; but the cushions in her flat were 'bright and garish, not at all the sort of thing anyone one knew would choose', and her kitchen was filthy. Her home was in Putney, and James thought 'it was perhaps where one would not care to have one's mother live'. And, of course, she called at the antique shop, though she had been told not to do so.

Meanwhile his friendship with Leonora developed. 'They had a cosy arrangement of telling each other of the day's happenings, either by meeting or by telephone.' 'Sometimes James would tell her about his childhood in America or read poetry to her while she toyed with a piece of tapestry work.'

James went off for his tour, and now trouble began. Phoebe went to the furniture depository to get the things James had promised her. She was told that Miss Eyre had taken the fruitwood mirror, but Phoebe had a few things sent to her cottage.

Phoebe and her friend Jennifer went to a teashop in Wigmore Street, into which Leonora (unknown to them by sight) came after a visit to her dentist – and was much annoyed to see Jennifer enjoying the last of her favourite chestnut cakes. By a charming coincidence (known only to us, the readers) a retired Brazilian diplomat watched the scene with amusement – we do not need to be told that he was Senhor MacBride Pereira, Dulcie's next-door neighbour (*NFR*), and we are not told. He is the only one of our old friends with a place in this book.

Phoebe called at the antique shop for news of James. She gathered the information that Leonora Eyre was a great friend of Humphrey's, and that James on his travels had picked up a companion, 'an American called Ned' – both facts were true, but falsely reassuring, for Phoebe imagined that neither Ned nor Leonora would be emotionally interesting to James. Humphrey decided that Phoebe was James's mistress, and looked forward to telling Leonora; this he did while they were having supper after the opera. It had been *Tosca*, and Humphrey, himself entirely unmusical, thought it rather second rate of Leonora to admire Puccini, who was at that time not much esteemed.

Leonora, so Humphrey thought, took the news very calmly, pretending not to be surprised, but she was shocked into action. She sat down at her desk and wrote a note to ask the tenant on the upper floor to vacate her flat at the end of the month. Then she intended to move in James's furniture from the store where he had meant to leave it until he found a new flat. When she heard Phoebe had a few things she determined to take them also.

James and Ned have seemed to other readers as well as myself to be a sort of Jekyll and Hyde – though here detached into two characters. Perhaps James (Jekyll) has not enough personality allotted to him. Barbara deals with his love-life briefly, modestly and explicitly. First we see him attracting the attention of 'a tall man with a slightly raffish air', and, though he rejects his proposition, 'who knows what might have happened' had there not been an interruption? James is an orphan, and Humphrey does not concern himself with his private life; if James has any affairs we also know nothing about them. With Leonora his relations are purely platonic; with Phoebe the affair was almost an accident, a collision; later it was 'like an amusing unreal game, so far removed from his everyday life that he could not feel his usual guilt'. The word 'usual' seems to imply affairs of one sort or another. With Ned we are shown the moments before, in a stuffy hotel room in Lisbon: 'What are we waiting for?' said Ned. On another occasion we see them after the event, in 'Ned's pad' near the Brompton Oratory.

'But this doesn't *feel* like England, does it...?' Ned stretched himself out on a synthetic black fur rug.
'No, it doesn't feel like anywhere,' James agreed.
'And yet it's *everywhere*.'*

Ned quoted no more Donne, knowing it would be thrown away on James: 'with him there could be none of the pleasure of flinging quotations back and forth at each other'.†

Indeed 'Jimmie was a sweet boy', but when Ned had successfully got him away from Leonora he began to be bored, and ceased to be faithful. James had a nice face and voice, and beautiful feet, but was not really an interesting companion; and like Leonora he had no sense of humour. Ned, though untruthful, unkind and utterly selfish, was intellectually very much the superior.

Leonora very easily evicted her tenant, for the excellent old lady (the only character in the book who ever goes to church) wished to retire to a home run by nuns where she could take her own furniture. 'Mrs Ainger' had told her about it – one imagines it

---

*For love, all love of other sights controules,
  And makes one little roome an everywhere.
†And yet James read poetry to Leonora – nineteeth-century poetry, I am inclined to guess.

was the admirable Sophia (*UA*) for Barbara was nothing if not economical, and liked to get the last drop out of her characters. The furniture in Phoebe's care presented a more difficult problem. Leonora thought (and she was not far wrong) that the liaison sounded rather sordid and unworthy, and could mean little to James. She obtained Phoebe's address from the furniture depository and went down in a Green Line bus to ask Phoebe to return the things. The appearance of the cottage fully confirmed her idea of the squalor of the affair. No one was at home, but a neighbour, Rose Culver, offered Leonora tea at her own cottage.

Several young people came to see Miss Sharpe, said Rose Culver. Leonora felt happily that James might only be one of many, and boasted rather unbecomingly of their friendship. 'We're very close.'

This is quite unlike her (and I am afraid it was put into her mouth in order to provoke the reply). But perhaps she realized that all her conduct that day had been more than usually lacking in subtlety.

Rose Culver was suddenly moved to prophesy: 'The odd thing about men is that one never really knows. . . . Just when you think they're close they suddenly go off.'

This starts a depressing train of thought. Leonora for a moment almost contemplated marriage. 'Quietly in London' – a sensible way of getting married and the most comfortable for the contracting parties. But so often the phrase covers up things that need covering up: a previous elopement (like that of Wickham and Lydia in *Pride and Prejudice*); a premature pregnancy; family disapproval; or the need to find a clergyman who is prepared to marry a divorced person in church. None of these conditions would apply in this case, only the extreme unsuitability of the couple, and the unconcealable difference in age.

Leonora, however, merely sent a note to Miss Sharpe asking when she might call to collect James's things. Phoebe replied (in a cheap, brown envelope) that she would not give them up until James asked her.

[117]

Not at all used to this sort of treatment, Leonora rang up Humphrey at the antique shop. Selfish (as people at the telephone so often are), she told his assistant that her call was urgent; in consequence, too weak to ask her to ring back later, he lost two valuable customers. His first thought was, reasonably, that it was a storm in a teacup; his next that Leonora must not be upset. He offered to drive her down to Phoebe's cottage and take the things. He had the faint, unworthy hope that Leonora might go too far and alienate James; then there might be a chance for him.

'I am James's uncle,' he told Phoebe, and added (not very explicitly) that he had 'offered' to collect the furniture. Leonora did not even get out of the car.

James returned from Portugal, and settled meekly into the flat above Leonora's, where all his things were carefully arranged – though the fruitwood mirror seems to have been hung below in Leonora's hall. The other people in his love-life were well out of the way: Phoebe was in Majorca with the money she had earned out of Anthea Wedge; Ned was in Oxford with friends, and perhaps was working on his thesis on Keats's minor poems. All for the moment was peace.

The disruptive Ned came on a Sunday afternoon, when James was in bed with a cold. He was received by Leonora, who at once knew that he was far more of a danger than Phoebe could ever have been. 'This was something she had always been afraid of in her relationship with James.' She began to think of ways in which the three of them might associate harmoniously together.

Ned stroked an alabaster dove on the mantelpiece, a present James had given her, and quoted:

> 'I had a dove and the sweet dove died;
> And I have thought it died of grieving . . .'

'Ah, yes, of course, that sad little poem,' said Leonora, who had quite forgotten it.

Ned went on, giving it a curious emphasis:

'O, what could it *grieve* for? Its feet were *tied*
With a single knot of my *own hand's* weaving.'

Leonora felt there was something sinister and obscure about the poem, as indeed there was. After Ned had gone 'the poem lingered in her mind. Would other people – would James himself – see their relationship like that?' she wondered.

The fight between her and Ned had begun, and we can have no doubt how it will end. Humphrey thinks: 'How much more sensible it would be for her to admit defeat and give up.'

She had a luncheon party for James and Ned, with Humphrey and Liz as the other guests – it left her more uneasy. A visit to Keats's house with the two young men showed her to be even more unwanted by James and Ned; the latter treated her as an elderly woman, as soon tired by exertion as his own mother.

Growing unhappiness and more acute awareness of the differences in age between her and her companions made her feel a sympathy very unlike her for another middle-aged woman, the only other visitor to the house, who wore a pixie hood and carried a string bag full of books on top of which lay the brightly coloured packet of frozen dinner for one! 'Leonora could see the artistically delineated slices of beef with dark brown gravy, a little round Yorkshire pudding, two mounds of mashed potato and brilliantly green peas.' Leonora, who herself was a great tin opener, had no right, anyway, to feel contemptuous of 'any body who could live this way'. One might prefer for oneself a lightly boiled egg or a baked potato – but the 'frozen dinner' would at least be safer than Leonora's tinned prawns or lobster.

'She saw the woman going home to a cosy solitude, her dinner heated up in twenty-five minutes with no bother or preparation, books to read, and a visit to Keats's house to cherish.'

The afternoon ended in 'Ned's pad', and Ned again treated Leonora as an elderly lady, and telephoned to order a taxi for her as she looked tired; she had expected James to run her home. This was James's first victory, said Ned, to whom it was really due.

[119]

Leonora now saw that she was a bad third; her only plan was to wait, and there would be no more threesomes. Unfortunately for her there would be no more cosy solitude either. One of the things James had taken from her was 'the pleasure of being alone, which she had enjoyed before she met him'. She even encouraged dull friends, like the depressing Liz and Meg. She was doomed to quite a long period of accidie – a state that generally passes or becomes lighter in the end, though there is seldom much that unoccupied people can do about it. No work of any sort had any appeal for her.

Ned's victory was complete. James found a flat in Chelsea and had his furniture moved, including the fruitwood mirror that Leonora had hoped to keep, not only for its associations, but also for the flattering reflection that she saw in it. The move had long ago been planned, but she may have hoped that her sharp practice in taking the things from the store and from Phoebe might have kept him under her roof – and but for Ned it might have done. 'Life is cruel and we do *terrible* things to each other,' said Ned, with tears in his eyes. 'That's what love is, hurting and being hurt.' But he encouraged James to drop Leonora as soon as he could.

James, however, will be 'no exception to the rule that nobody tired of Ned before he had tired of them'. James was always there – and there were other lovers.

In May Ned called on Leonora to say goodbye; he was going back to America. He said that his mother needed him, but his own need was to disentangle himself from James and other complications. Rather complacently he offered to give James back to her, but neither James nor Leonora feels that it is possible for them to go on again. The sweet dove of friendship has died, killed by kindness.

Not a happy ending on the whole. The impervious Ned, after violent scenes with James and a patched-up reconciliation, will go home cheerfully to America. There he will certainly find his mother, about whom he professed to be anxious, in perfect health; and probably his university will reward his thesis with a PhD. Humphrey, though still pursuing, will continue to be disappointed, until Leonora gently drops out of his life. She had bought new clothes, and feels revived by the spring; but the winter has been hard and has taken its toll of her – she is more than a year older. James, escaped from her toils and from other complications, is only twenty-five, and has life in front of him.

It is a sad book about a sad year. We can feel that it is largely because of Leonora's controlled and planned existence that she has made herself so unhappy, and that so many readers dislike her, in spite of her charm and good will – and sometimes on account of them. People are not comfortable with her.

This is the author's best book up till now, but there is something lacking that was never lacking in the 'canon' – it is the element of desirable life. It is not necessary (I think) that every novel should include at least one character with whom the reader can identify, but perhaps there should be at least some moment or experiences which the reader would like to share. The only such moments are those of the woman in the pixie hood, when she has taken off her wet things and sits down with a book, while she warms up her 'frozen dinner for one' – and even that is not an attractive meal.

12

Quartet in Autumn

Quartet in Autumn, though written after *The Sweet Dove Died*, was published before it, the first novel to appear after Barbara's rediscovery. It seems better to place it here, and to ignore the accidents of publication. *The Sweet Dove* follows more closely upon the 'canon', having been written in a world still recognizably the same, and less distressed by inflation. It has also a 'muted' love-story – a theme entirely absent from *Quartet*.

As always, there is in both these books the same limited canvas, and the acute, often ironic observation to which the 'canon' has made us accustomed; but in neither of them is there much of the same cosiness. *Quartet* is darker and sadder than any other of Barbara's novels – it was begun after her first cancer operation – but it is her strongest, finest work.

Edwin, Norman, Marcia and Letty work in the same office; their work is even less defined than that of Prudence (*JP*), and it is evidently unimportant. When Marcia and Letty reach retiring age they will not be replaced. The two men remain and are quite sufficient staff for a department that is to be closed when they also retire. Many novels have been written about the old but not very many about the ageing, such as these, all of whom are just on one or the other side of retirement. It is comforting to remember that the author had a very cosy and agreeable retirement in prospect.

Between them the four reveal to us some of the ways in which the world has gone down since the time of the 'canon'. Norman, who visits a supermarket on his way to work, tells us of rising prices, particularly of butter beans. This would not be likely to affect the people in *The Sweet Dove*. Nor would they notice the changes in the Church, by which Edwin is much distressed. He regretfully remembers the crowds collected at a lunch-time mass by Father Thames or Father Bode (*GB*), and feels lucky to find a few people at an evening sung mass, even if some of them are black. He has a tower of strength in 'Father G.' (Father Gellibrand). Other clergy are often 'trendy', long-haired, dressed in jeans, and more likely to welcome guitars in church, or a talk about the Third World, than to hold solemn evensong and benediction.

Characters in *The Sweet Dove* give us the impression that they are not likely to care for the novels that were the staple of the circulating libraries (Leonora takes *In Memoriam* to read in the train), but Letty, once a keen novel-reader, 'had come to realize that the position of an unmarried, unattached, ageing woman is of no interest whatever to the writer of modern fiction', and cannot find anyone to identify herself with in these books. And yet one wonders if she would greatly care for this novel, in which she figures. Marcia is too near to madness to belong to any period. She has suffered 'major surgery' and had 'something removed' (a breast) – she is proud of this distinction, and cherishes a platonic devotion to her surgeon, though that is but a small part of her eccentricities. One is sometimes tempted to feel that the whole world is, as she is later said to be, in 'a terminal situation'.

There is no sort of companionship and no hostility between the four, no common interest and no rivalry. At first Marcia seems to have felt a faint sympathy for Norman, and when she made her will before her 'serious operation' she left him her house. Most of the sympathy died away, but she did not trouble to change her will, indeed she had only uncared for cousins to whom to leave it.

A note of Barbara's (*mutatis mutandis*) found later expression in the gentleness of Letty.

... the unmarried middle-aged women in the office. Both have had affairs of some kind, but now they can express love only through a tenderness and solicitude towards each other, 'Let me make you a cup of tea,' 'Shouldn't you go home?' These feelings that should have been directed towards husband or child.*

Letty and Marcia had had no affairs of any sort, but 'In such circumstances women may feel a certain unsentimental tenderness towards each other, expressed in small gestures of solicitude. It was Letty who said, "You look tired – shall I make you a cup of tea?" Marcia, glancing sharply at Letty, thought, she's like an old sheep, but she means well. . . .' A surprising note of charity in Marcia.

We see the four together in the office, but apart when they are out of it. They do not meet on their journeys to and fro, in the evenings, or on their holidays. Sometimes at lunch-time they go, severally, to the local library: Edwin has gone there to check the careers of clergymen in Crockford, Norman and Marcia for warmth – she will also collect pamphlets setting out the various services offered to the elderly, though she will never avail herself of any of them. Letty alone wants something to read and, disappointed in fiction, she may take a biography. She is the only one who lunches at the Rendezvous, where office workers have hurried meals, such as 'macaroni au gratin with chips, and a glass of water'. The others usually bring something with them to the office, and Marcia makes instant coffee for herself and Norman, for it is cheaper to buy a big tin.

Norman is sour and pessimistic, Marcia almost mad. Edwin and Letty are the happy two. Letty had a bed-sitting-room in the house of an elderly woman. 'It was a comfortable enough life, if a little sterile, perhaps, even deprived. But deprivation implied once having had something to be deprived of.' 'Love was a mystery she had never experienced. As a young woman she had wanted to love,

*A Very Private Eye, p. 270.

[124]

had felt she ought to, but it had not come about.' In this she is not unique in Barbara's books; Mildred (*EW*) had never loved and we do not know that she ever will, though she will marry. Now Letty gave no more thought to it. As a girl she had taken a secretarial course, and vaguely expected to marry some day – but in this, as in everything, she seemed to trail behind her friend Marjorie. It was assumed that on retirement she would share a cottage in the country with Marjorie, now a widow; in her holidays they had sometimes gone together on package tours to Spain or Italy, unlike her colleagues, who never went abroad.

The course of her life was suddenly disturbed, but she accepted the disturbance without great anxiety. First, Marjorie became engaged to her new vicar; she expected to sell her cottage and to move into the vicarage, and would have no home for Letty – but she suggested that (with her influence) she could get Letty into an old people's home in the village. Letty did not fancy the idea and preferred to wait and see; she might decide to remain in London.

A second and more immediate change was now forced upon her. Her landlady retired into just such an old people's home and sold the house, and the tenants with it, to Mr Jacob Olatunde, a Nigerian and apparently head of a religious sect. Edwin had told her that 'splendid West Africans' came to his church, and did very well in the sanctuary; Letty was to find that their noise was intolerable in the house, and the smell of their cooking was overpowering. 'How had it come about that she, an English-woman born at Malvern in 1914 of middle-class English parents, should find herself in this room in London surrounded by enthusiastic, shouting, hymn-singing Nigerians?' It must have been all the more bitter because she, unlike Norman, was carefully free of all racial prejudice. She thought: 'It must surely be because she had not married.' She had made the mistake to think that love was 'a necessary ingredient for marriage'.

Edwin kindly made overtures for her to an old lady at one of the churches that he frequented, and within six weeks Letty was installed in Miss Pope's back room. The room was pleasant, though the West Hampstead neighbourhood was unattractive. Edwin hoped that, like Miss Pope, Letty would fall into the rhythm of the Church's year, though she was now a very infrequent church-goer. At Christmas her chief care was that no one should pity her because she had no engagements for the day – and in peaceful solitude she got through the day more easily than her former colleagues, for whom engagements had been found. She cheered up when she remembered that the Kensington sales started on the day after Boxing Day.

'Roll on retirement,' Norman was accustomed to say, but the women reached retiring age first. The unnamed organization for which they had done their equally unspecified work thought a lunch-time party appropriate. The (acting) deputy assistant director is thought important enough to make the presentation speech, and neither he nor anyone else seems to know quite what Marcia and Letty have done all those years, but it emerges that they will not be replaced, and that the department to which they were attached will be closed when their male colleagues retire. It is a picture of anonymity and uselessness; they seem never to have existed. When we see Marcia and Letty on the first day of their liberty, the first feeling is that of a vacuum.

Nevertheless Letty tried to enter into the life of the North-west London suburb where now she lived. We see her shuffling round the stations of the Cross one Lenten evening, cheered by Easter, chilly in church at Whitsun when the heating had been turned down; warmly welcoming Edwin when he appeared one day, and helping to sort out clothes sent in response to an appeal for aged refugees. She did not yet understand what it was all about, but she began to feel settled. When Marjorie was jilted by her vicar, it did not seem likely that Letty would go back to her old plan of sharing the cottage. She wanted to take time and think it over.

Letty is the pleasantest character of the four, the least assertive and, though her reading matter is rather inferior, the least unlike the author; all meetings seem to go off more peacefully if she is present.

Edwin was the most fortunate of the four, and had a small house of his own and was quite a capable cook. For some years he had been a widower. One evening he had found Phyllis, his wife, unconscious in the kitchen, when she had been about to put a shepherd's pie in the oven. He had a married daughter and grandchildren living not far away; he was thus provided for, in a sense; no social worker would have the right to bother him, and he would pose no problem to anyone on holidays. In fact his daughter and her husband were thinking they would like to go to Spain in a year or two, when the children were older. If they were worried about Edwin it was quite unnecessary, he could take very good care of himself. He did not at all miss his wife and found a little family life went a long way.

He was an excellent churchman; his great friend was 'Father G.', vicar of a church near Clapham Common, where Edwin was Master of the Ceremonies and a member of the Parochial Church Council. This gave him what would have been quite a full life even if he had not his office, for he liked going round London and Greater London sampling the churches. Even, on occasion, he deserted his post in his own parish to hear a high mass elsewhere on a Sunday. It was his great pleasure in the lunch-time break to study the service lists of nearby churches or their parish magazines; sometimes with a bus he could get a little farther, as far as All Saints, Margaret Street. If there were a lunch-time mass anywhere he would find out and attend it. On the eves of feast-days he would go to churches for their patronal festivals. His Christmas plans were very different from Letty's.

Today, December 27th, was St John the Evangelist and there should be a good High Mass this evening at St John's over the other side of the common.... Then there was the day after, December 28th, Holy Innocents – he'd try to get over to Hammersmith for that. People didn't seem to realize what a lot was going on after Christmas, quite apart from the day itself.

Moreover he had to keep Father G., in the right way. All very well to introduce 'Series Three', though people would not like standing to pray and the 'Kiss of Peace' was not practical in an almost empty church and 'nobody standing next to anybody to make any kind of gesture' – though there were plenty of people to do it in the sanctuary, and one can imagine that the 'splendid West Africans' would love it. But there must not be 'a horde of boys and girls brandishing guitars' on a Sunday evening. Some order and decency remained, though there was no longer the sympathetic climate of twenty years ago, when the Church knew better days. Edwin, however, had sufficiently moved with the times to tell Letty that 'very early services were rather old-fashioned now and that an evening mass was the thing'.

Norman was a sour, irritable little man. He went to visit his brother-in-law Ken in hospital, though his sister (Ken's wife) was dead and their only child had emigrated to New Zealand. He thought he was being dutiful, and that Ken had no one. In fact it was Norman who had no one, whereas Ken was planning to marry a woman with whom he hoped to set up a driving-school. The brothers-in-law had little to say to each other, and Norman returned crossly to his bed-sitting-room in Kilburn.

He was full of pessimistic predictions; they were all in danger of 'falling through the net of the Welfare State', of being found dead of hypothermia or starvation. Though he once picked up a brochure and said he would like to go to Greece, his last holiday had been spent on a wet coach tour in the West Country, and the next was just idled away; he did not know what to do with himself when he was not working. He spent Christmas Day with Ken and his future wife; they gave him a very good meal, but he returned to his bed-sitting-room 'quite well satisfied with his lot'. At the end of the book he was surprised to find that Marcia had left him her house. After some repairs it would be a 'desirable property', for the neighbourhood was 'going up'. Out of gratitude he tried to invent a flattering portrait of her. But his main satisfaction lay in the fact that he had the choice to live in it or to sell it; he could influence the lives of the neighbours by his decision, and even be a nuisance to some of them.

Marcia is Barbara's one tragic heroine. She had a house, though it was in very bad repair, and the grass grew high in her garden. Her mother had lately died at an advanced age, so also her cat, Snowy. She was usually dressed in a strange assortment of clothes and had dyed her hair a harsh brown for the last thirty years, neglecting the roots. She was a natural solitary, seldom idle for she had invented odd employments for herself. 'A woman can always find plenty to occupy her time,' she said. She would fold nylon bags (of which she had amassed a quantity), arranging them by size and carefully putting them away where no one could suffocate inside them, though no children ever entered the house. Or she would rearrange the cupboard where she had stored a great variety of food, ranging from soups to vine leaves, or tapioca pudding. She frequently added to them 'in case of emergency', but hardly ever touched them. Norman had warned her that one might not have the strength to open them – and in fact when we do see her for once trying to open a tin of 'luncheon meat', 'the metal tab broke off and she lacked the strength to manoeuvre it any further'. She lived on cups of tea and an occasional biscuit. She never found the time to dust her house and its heavy furniture, or to do anything for her grass-grown garden beyond visiting from time to time a shed, where she had a large collection of milk bottles – these she hardly ever returned, fearing that an emergency of some sort might arise when the milkman would say (as during the war) 'no bottle no milk'.

The great moment of her life had been her mastectomy operation. Mr Strong, the surgeon, became her hero – and she looked back to hospital with a nostalgia almost as great as that of Maggie in *Little Dorrit*.

A typical scene in her kitchen is this:

She supposed she should have something to eat, but it was a bother to cook anything and she didn't want to disturb her supply of tins. So she just made a cup of tea and put plenty of sugar in it, like the tea at the hospital. 'Cup of tea, Miss Ivory? Sugar, dear?' It gave Marcia a warm feeling to remember those days and that nice woman – Nancy, they called her – coming round with the tea.

This was 'the element of desirable life' in her existence. Norman seems to have had none.

She was the bane of the social worker, Janice Bramber, no doubt a worthy young woman who did voluntary work at the Centre, and could not understand that Marcia only wanted to be left in peace. 'Some of us at the Centre have been worrying about the lonely ones,' is her opening and most unfortunate remark. 'Some of us' almost invariably denotes prigs or busybodies, as Marcia may not have noticed; but she was furious at being called 'a lonely one', and regarded with horror an invitation to 'come along to a get-together at the Centre'. Janice complained to a colleague: 'People like that don't seem to *want* to be helped.' She could not understand Marcia's fierce independence, and did not know that, having for years collected pamphlets, she did not need any information about reduced prices available to pensioners. 'So many of them don't *know* what they're entitled to, how people are *falling over backwards* to help them' was the social workers' cry. But people commonly 'fall over backwards' to be a nuisance.

Janice Bramber's efforts are seconded by Nigel and Priscilla, a young couple who have bought the house next door to Marcia's, and have a patio and other signs of contemporary elegance. The feel they should 'do something' about her; Marcia repulses Nigel's offer to mow her grass, but does accept their invitation to luncheon on Christmas Day, when she hardly eats a thing.

If she has otherwise 'fallen through the net of the Welfare State', she is devoted to the Health Service. She went with enthusiasm to out-patients at the hospital when she was due for a check-up. She arrived early and snubbed all attempts at conversation by other patients. She had put on new underwear for the occasion – she had a whole drawer full, reserved for hospital wear. A young houseman examined her and told her that she was too thin and ought to eat more. 'I think perhaps somebody should keep an eye on you,' he said kindly. Marcia took this from him as she would not from a social worker – hospital was different. But she was not any more inclined to be obedient and try to eat.

She made a pilgrimage by bus to look at Mr Strong's house in Dulwich – the family was away for August, but it was enough to have seen it. She went home and boiled herself an egg and made a cup of tea – she had been told to eat more. It must be seldom that she bought anything fresh like an egg; but at our first meeting with her she had uncharacteristically brought to the office a sandwich of lettuce and tomato. Her shopping basket usually contained nothing but tins.

A year later she told another doctor: 'I've never been a big eater. But nobody can say that I don't keep a good table. You should just see my store-cupboard.' Very little, however, leaves the cupboard.

'I don't know what Mr Strong is going to say when he sees you looking so thin,' said the doctor, and the magic of that name made Marcia promise to go home at once and cook something. But on arriving home after a bus journey, on which she had been conjecturing what Mr Strong would have for dinner, she felt another urge to go on pilgrimage to Dulwich to see what vegetables were in the kitchen garden.

Janice, the social worker, after a fortnight in Greece, went to see Marcia. She could not get in, and was alarmed at the sight of several new milk bottles – through the glass panel of the back door she saw Marcia sitting humped at the table. By a coincidence – I think the only one that Barbara ever allowed herself as part of a plot – Edwin decided to look in that day, and brought Father G. with him. Marcia's parish priest was not likely to keep an eye on her – 'Trendy Tony' went in for rock-and-roll and extempore prayers rather than for parish visiting.

No one could have been more useful at this juncture – Janice was left out and the two men took over, Father G. was used to visiting people *in extremis*, and rather preferred them that way; and Edwin in the past had had to have his wife taken away by ambulance to the hospital. Marcia, who had always wanted to ride in an ambulance, was not conscious enough to enjoy the fulfilment of her ambition. 'Unreachable inside a room' – Barbara quotes her friend Philip Larkin.

In hospital Marcia lay silent, hardly aware that flowers had been sent her from her three office colleagues, from Janice, and from Priscilla and Nigel. Letty also sent lavender water, and she was freshened up for Mr Strong's visit. The young houseman reported her as being in a 'terminal condition'. Her thoughts were confused, but she was able to smile when Mr Strong came, and died happy.

Edwin had volunteered to be considered as 'next of kin'. They all went to the crematorium and Father G. read the service. Finally the three survivors tidied up the house and drank a bottle of Cyprus sherry discovered in a cupboard – they thought it was what 'Marcia would have wished'; the dead seem always to approve of what the survivors find convenient.

It is a fine, uncomfortable book, and yet there is a ray of hope. Some people will have a dreary old age, others will die of hypothermia or otherwise 'fall through the net of the Welfare State' – or strangle in it. These four have a sturdy independence; none of them whines or moans. Loneliness (such a bugbear in the minds of social workers) seldom afflicts them. All of them have the wireless and (when she is with Miss Pope) Letty has also television – and yet none of them is an addict, with ears or eyes glued to the box. Edwin and Norman are glad to escape from such family ties as they have. Letty stays with Marjorie in the country, but will not think of retiring to an old people's home in the village. 'The church people' suggested that Marcia should join a coach trip to Westcliff on Sea ('Much nicer than Southend, dear'). She did not wish to do so, nor to follow any of Janice Bramber's suggestions. 'I can never understand why people have to leave their homes,' she said. 'When you're older you don't really need holidays.'

Edwin with his church activities, Letty with her reading (once she had given up sociology and its tiresome jargon) have positive happiness, such as people can enjoy at any time of life. Letty also enjoys nature, even the little bits of it she sees in London. In the 'real' country there are such unpleasant sights as animals run over on the road. Norman and Marcia are at least not unhappy in their odd lives – they would not wish to change them.

These people reassure us that the world is not, after all, in a 'terminal situation'. They will not be cowed by friend or foe into giving up their liberty. No kind of persuasion will break their obstinacy. One great advantage they have over many people in their state of life – and of better-placed people too – is that they are without envy of more fortunate people, and without any feeling that they have been unjustly neglected. Their way of life may be threatened by 'do-gooders', but they can repel them. Their idiosyncracy will triumph over any sort of totalitarianism – it is weaker souls who are 'so grateful', and make things worthwhile for the social workers.

13

A Few Green Leaves

This is Barbara's farewell to her readers, revised not long before her death and published shortly after it. A gentle, kindly book with less of the melancholy that marked the two novels which preceded it. The pattern of her evolution is now complete, and we can see that her life was shaped for her more precisely than she can have known until her last years. In better times and in juvenile high spirits she had begun on her career as a novelist with *Some Tame Gazelle*, imagining herself, her sister and many of her friends and acquaintances in comfortable middle age. Then in the lean years that immediately followed the war she wrote *Excellent Women*, a work redolent of the kitchen sink. In the better days that came after, beginning with *Jane and Prudence*, when life was still not so easy, and going on through the novels of the 'canon', she was a domestic historian of her times, as well as the historian of her people and happenings – but continually light-hearted.

Then followed the rejection of a book which, I have argued, was a blessing in disguise – if very thoroughly and unkindly disguised.

Thereafter something of her confidence was gone, and her high spirits as a writer had been damped; life also had brought disappointment. The next book she wrote (though not the next published) was *The Sweet Dove Died*, and here there is an after-taste of sadness. The world is less simple than that of the 'canon'. The characters, on the whole, are socially a little higher placed, and there is not much cosiness. It is a less virtuous world where nearly every character is out for something. They do not even trouble to exercise much subtlety about their designs or desires, and are more likely to hoodwink themselves than others. If others are taken in it is because their attention is elsewhere; the author is never taken in.

Quartet in Autumn feels like the end of a world – and a world not very like that of Barbara's previous novels; there is a sharp drop in the social level of the people since *The Sweet Dove*. Marcia (her finest, perhaps her only tragic character) is medically in a 'terminal condition'; and at first all four members of the quartet, whose last working hours are spent in an office far less refined than that of Prudence (*PJ*), do not seem to have much life ahead of them of the sort the superficial would call 'life'. But the stern obstinacy with which they resist well meaning (or institutional) help and advice secures for them an idiosyncratic independence and gives hope to us all. We can be grateful to them for their existence and their struggle. The 'deputy assistant director' of their place of work spoke more truly than he knew when, in his farewell speech, he called two of them 'the kind of people who work quietly and secretly, doing good by stealth' – even if the only good they did was to be there.

Now we have a last book, written after Barbara's rediscovery and in the certainty of publication. It has, perhaps, for this reason, a resumed cheerfulness, although she knew she could not have long to live. As it is set in a west Oxfordshire village (not unlike that of Finstock, to which she had now retired with her sister), the changes that the world has suffered are less keenly felt; we seem to have gone back a little in time.

We follow the life of the village from late April or early May until some time in the next February. Emma Howick, an anthropologist in her early thirties, who is staying in a cottage to write up her notes on a former project, conceived the idea of making a study of the village life – and is more like a working anthropologist than any other in Barbara's books, for her 'field' is the background to this book and she is really concerned with 'collective habits and social behaviour' more than with the investigation of individual oddities. We see the people and many of the events through Emma's eyes. We are assured by her friend and neighbour Gilbert Phelps* that Barbara resisted all temptations to put actual Finstock personalities into this book.

Change in the village is recorded by one or two of the older inhabitants – apart from changes that are self-evident. The family de Tankerville has sold the manor and is only represented by monuments in the church and a mausoleum. 'The last governess', Miss Vereker, is present as a living ghost in the reminiscences of Miss Olive Lee. The manor is now the property of Sir Miles Brambleton, who leaves everything in the hands of an agent, and takes little interest in the house, which he seldom visits, and none in the village or the church.

However, the traditional right of the villagers to walk in the grounds of the manor every year on Low Sunday is still respected, and this walk affords Emma a first view of all her neighbours. She begins to think that she may wish to study the village instead of merely writing up the notes she had accumulated before coming – 'something to do with attitudes towards almost everything you could think of in one of the new towns'.

'Some Observations on the Social Patterns of a West Oxfordshire Village', she typed. The walk had shown her that the higher gentry played no role. She thought of beginning with the Church, but soon observed that while the congregation in church was small and the rector, Tom Dagnall, not held of much account, the village flocked to the surgery on Mondays and Thursdays. The 'old' doctor, Dr Gellibrand, brother of 'Father G.' (QA), and his domineering wife Christabel were the first people of the place – she even tried to usurp the vacant position of 'lady of the manor'.

The first event in the calendar of village life was 'Christabel G.'s' sherry party. Emma, 'even with her anthropological training', was not sure what this party was 'for'. We are told 'it was not so much to welcome newcomers... as to sort out in a

*The Life and Work of Barbara Pym, p. 38.

[136]

social way sheep from goats and pick out various likely people to "do" things in the village, above all to assist in the flower festival'.

The next 'event' was the jumble sale. Emma, like other people, took her offering of cast-off clothing to the rectory. The rector's sister told her, 'the village women have such marvellous things now. They wouldn't look at cast-offs – it's we who buy them.' There is no poverty any more.

Emma receives an invitation to the next event: a 'Coffee Morning and Bring-and-Buy Sale' held in their cottage by Miss Lee and Miss Grundy. We look into her notebook. *In aid of what?* This she never discovered. *Entrance*: the 15p included a cup of rather weak coffee and a biscuit – rather too many ladies were serving it. *Participants*: Men (none), Women (mixed). *Bring and Buy*: 'the bringing and buying, consisting as it did of people bringing what they had made and buying what somebody else had made, achieved a kind of village exchange system'. *The raffle*: an essential feature ('We always have one'). Adam Prince made an unexpected entry, bearing a bottle of wine for the raffle. He was a former Anglican priest who had 'gone over' to Rome, and was now a 'good food inspector', visiting provincial restaurants and reporting on them.

The Flower Festival followed – at the cost of the hurt feelings of at least one decorator (the rector's sister, as in *EW*). Christabel G. was in command, and the church looked lovely 'though not quite like a church'. Then the rector had his turn, leading the history society's summer excursion, consisting mainly of middle-aged and elderly women from neighbouring villages – 'Tom's history ladies', whose names were 'seven sweet symphonies' (Mary, Janet, Leila, Damaris, Ailsa, Myrtle and Hester), were the backbone of the society, but there were a few women from his own village – and again Adam Prince was the only man. They went by coach to a celebrated country house, and had tea in the grounds.

In early autumn there was a 'Hunger Lunch' – this also was held in Miss Lee's and Miss Grundy's cottage, the profits in aid of the Third World. Usually delicious home-baked bread was offered, but this time only a sliced loaf – as Dr G. observed, 25p 'seems a bit steep for a slice of pappy bread and a sliver of mouse trap' – for he and the rector are also present.

Miss Lee was the leader of a party to go round the manor, and told them more about Miss Vereker and the unattractive things for which she was famous. We already knew that she 'had a way with ewe mutton', and now we hear of her arrangements of fir-cones and wild grasses, and her blackberry wine.

The death of the village eccentric took place one evening when the light had failed.

Miss Lickerish had not bothered to put on the light at the normal time. She boiled a kettle on the fire and then sat in her chair with a cup of tea at her side and a cat on her knees. But some time during those dark hours the cat left her and sought the warmth of his basket, Miss Lickerish's lap having become strangely chilled.

Emma was soon at work on 'Funeral Customs in a Rural Community'. An extension of the obsequies was observed on the following Sunday when a group of mourners came to church. The rector pointed out that this gave a kind of continuity to village life.

The book ends with a lecture to the History Society by Dr G. – but although he exhibits a few antique surgical instruments, he develops his favourite theme that people ought to *walk* more.

Shortly before this event came the climax – in the penultimate position of a climax in Greek tragedy. Miss Vereker, 'the last governess', came unannounced on what was intended to be a day-trip, to revisit her former haunts. She lost her way in the woods, sat down and fell asleep – inadvertently discovering stones of the deserted medieval village, the object of the rector's years' long quest. There she was found by Emma and Avice Shrubsole, the wife of the 'young doctor' – and medieval and modern history are satisfactorily united.

The fundamental changes in the village are half-concealed

behind these 'events', which are repetitions almost unaltered of similar gatherings in the past. The big change at the manor had taken place too long ago to be felt by anyone except Miss Lee, but it must have been a change for the worse, from a family that cared for the place and people to a man generally absent, who seems only to come for Christmas or for a weekend house-party. The agent merely laughs when Emma asks for the 'estate carpenter'.

The village has grown; in particular there is 'a little cluster of bungalows' on the site formerly known as 'Sangreal Copse'. Apart from the manor there are only two handsome, good-sized houses; one belongs to Dr and Christabel G., the other is the rectory. The former is well kept and admirably furnished, as Christabel G. has both money and taste. The latter, though also beautiful, is very shabby as Daphne, the rector's sister, has neither. Avice Shrubsole, the 'young doctor's' wife, very much covets the rectory and makes ceaseless and rather crude attempts to get Tom Dagnall to give it up and move into a small house – a change that is now common in village life elsewhere.

Emma speculates about the village diet. 'What did people in the village eat? she wondered.'

Sunday evening supper would of course be lighter than the normal weekday meal, with husbands coming back from work.... [Some] would be taking out ready-prepared meals or even joints of meat from their freezers, or would have bought supper dishes at the supermarket with tempting titles and bright attractive pictures on the cover. Sometimes there might even be fish, for a man called round occasionally with fresh fish at the back of his van.

Adam Prince, who writes (professionally) about good food, tries to preserve civilized standards, and the strain keeps him awake at night. Dr G. almost cruelly tells him: 'Try not to be quite so critical – learn to like processed cheese and tea-bags and instant coffee, and beef-burgers and fish fingers too – most of the people in the village live on such things and they're none the worse for it.' One ought, no doubt, to be able to consume such things (though the 'young doctor' would greatly disapprove); but it would be dreadful to like them, and it would be the end of Adam's profession.

No one seems to think of eating fruit or vegetables, apart from Magdalen Raven, mother-in-law of Martin Shrubsole (the 'young doctor') who is strictly dieted by her son-in-law, who conscientiously does all he can to prolong her life because he would be so greatly relieved if she were to die. In consequence she is hardly ever allowed to eat anything that she likes. Daphne, the sister of the rector, is continually pining for Greece – and the imitations of Greek food that she gives him sound even nastier than the original. When she is absent he is left to his own resources: 'the packet of savoury rice, the ever-useful fish fingers or the miniature steak and kidney pie, heated up in its little dish'. Adam Prince advises him to 'enlist the help of the ladies' – in fact to put a letter in the parish magazine asking them to take pity on him and invite him to an occasional meal – 'whatever you are having yourselves'. Nearly everyone is tempted to make some use of 'convenience' foods: even Emma, who is a good cook, once resorts to a tinned rice pudding.

The change in the village that Dr G. most deplores is that from the 'good old days' of the 1930s before the introduction of the National Health Service, and before everyone had a motor car. Then people would walk to surgery from the next village; but now even children expected to be driven to school. The station yard was full of cars: people went by train to work in Oxford or even in London, returning in the evening. There was a cottage garden crowded with derelict motor cars, and this odd kind of cemetery was opposite the church. 'A Note on the Significance of the Abandoned Motor Car in a West Oxfordshire Village' might pin it down, thought Emma.

The book has the 'muted love-story' that occurs in all Barbara's novels except *Quartet*; in fact it may be said to have two. Emma sees a former lover (or is that too strong a word for him?) on television, and writes to him on the spur of the moment. He makes a rather unsuccessful visit, but then comes back for some weeks and takes a cottage in the woods, as a quiet place in which to finish some work. Emma does a little cooking for him, but is not greatly disappointed when he leaves the village for his new house in Islington and his reconciled wife Claudia. But his presence has stirred the jealousy of Tom Dagnall, the rector – a confirmed bachelor living with his sister Daphne. She eventually leaves him, and finds herself sharing a house with a friend in Birmingham, when she had hoped for a white cottage near the Aegean.

Emma's mother Beatrix (an Oxford don) happens to visit the village when Daphne has come back for a few days, and is extremely anxious that she should not settle down again with her brother and make him less marriageable, for she intends him to marry Emma. Her very unsubtle tactics remind us of Sophia Ainger's attempt to keep Rupert Stonebird for her sister (*UA*), but are more persistent, and are perhaps the most amusing thing in the book. It is evident that Tom and Emma will have to be rather more co-operative if the plan is to succeed. The question is left open, and the reader may answer it as he pleases – and I think the author wished him to please himself. Against the marriage: one does not see what friends Emma will have in the village – Avice Shrubsole and Adam Prince are not quite good enough. For it: Emma may bring it off just to show (herself, for that is all that matters) that she can if she chooses.

Tom is as 'moderate' a clergyman as Nicholas Cleveland (*JP*), and not in the least 'trendy'; no guitar or thurible has ever entered his church. He is an antiquarian, with his interest mainly focused on what he calls the 'D.M.V.' – a deserted mediaeval village, whose site was not located in the woods till Miss Vereker sat down in it. His other great interest was in the late seventeenth-century law about burial in wool.

Dr G. was more often sought for advice than the rector, for he could write a prescription, that imagined passport to health. In fact his favourite piece of advice to women patients with a tendency to hypochondria was: 'buy yourself a new hat' – a thing none of them had worn for years.

Christabel G. ruled that part of the doctor's life that was not protected by his surgery, but Tom Dagnall's study was no protection against his sister Daphne. It seems to Emma that whenever there are two people in a household one is usually a tyrant. Miss Olive Lee, an old inhabitant, bosses Miss Flavia Grundy, who lives with her. Emma and the 'good food inspector' are lucky enough to live alone and like it. Many people in this village are dominated by an alarming cleaning woman 'Dyer by name and Dire by nature'.

Emma and Adam are the people most contented with their lot. Daphne is pining for Greece; Magdalen Raven for sugar; Miss Lee for the 'good old days' of the Tankervilles and Miss Vereker; Miss Grundy for solemn evensong and incense; Avice Shrubsole for a larger house.

Miss Lee cannot recover 'the days that are no more', but perhaps gets back into some sort of past in her holiday at a 'Christian guesthouse' in the West Country – it is the dismal Anchorage where Dulcie and Viola once spent a night (*NFR*). Miss Grundy spends a few days in London visiting congenial churches, though 'the middle summer months were not the best for festivals'. Daphne went to Greece; Adam wandered round the Dordogne in search of truffles, others went farther afield; but Tom and Emma stayed at home.

One likes to think that the 'imaginary village' is not too great a feat of the imagination, but has resemblances to places well known to the author, even though they have passed through her imagination. It is a consoling book, an epilogue to her work – not to be judged by quite the same criteria as her novels, for it is a chronicle in which people and happenings occur without a strict pattern. It would be better if there were no sort of love-story, however 'muted', and Emma's detachment were more complete, for this apology for a plot invites criticism which the book should have evaded.

And though we must entirely believe Gilbert Phelps's assertion that no Finstock personalities have been 'put into' it, some local atmosphere must pervade the book, and it is understandable that many of Barbara's readers have made pilgrimages to the place where she spent her last years, and some of the happiest times of her life.

The Novels of Barbara Pym

Some Tame Gazelle, Jonathan Cape, 1950.
Excellent Women, Jonathan Cape, 1952.
Jane and Prudence, Jonathan Cape, 1953.
Less than Angels, Jonathan Cape, 1955.
A Glass of Blessings, Jonathan Cape, 1958.
No Fond Return of Love, Jonathan Cape, 1961.
Quartet in Autumn, Macmillan, 1977.
The Sweet Dove Died, Macmillan, 1978.
A Few Green Leaves, Macmillan, 1980.
An Unsuitable Attachment, Macmillan, 1982.
Crampton Hodnet, Macmillan, 1985.